The Savvy Principal

What Streetwise Principals Know

Jody Capelluti

ROWMAN & LITTLEFIELD EDUCATION
A division of
ROWMAN & LITTLEFIELD
Lanham • Boulder • New York • Toronto • Plymouth, UK

Published by Rowman & Littlefield Education
A division of Rowman & Littlefield
4501 Forbes Boulevard, Suite 200, Lanham, Maryland 20706
www.rowman.com

10 Thornbury Road, Plymouth PL6 7PP, United Kingdom

Copyright © 2014 by Jody Capelluti

All rights reserved. No part of this book may be reproduced in any form or by any electronic or mechanical means, including information storage and retrieval systems, without written permission from the publisher, except by a reviewer who may quote passages in a review.

British Library Cataloguing in Publication Information Available

Library of Congress Cataloging-in-Publication Data

Capelluti, Jody.
 The savvy principal : what streetwise principals know / Jody Capelluti.
 pages cm.
 Includes index.
 ISBN 978-1-61048-625-5 (cloth : alk. paper) — ISBN 978-1-61048-626-2 (pbk. : alk. paper) — ISBN 978-1-61048-627-9 (electronic) 1. School principals—Handbooks, manuals, etc. 2. School management and organization. 3. Communication in education. 4. Educational leadership. I. Title.
 LB2831.9.C34 2013
 371.2'012—dc23

2013031348

∞™ The paper used in this publication meets the minimum requirements of American National Standard for Information Sciences Permanence of Paper for Printed Library Materials, ANSI/NISO Z39.48-1992.

Printed in the United States of America

Contents

Preface	vii
Introduction	xi
Acknowledgments	xvii
1 Selecting the Right Boss and Community	1
2 Where You Choose to Live Is a Life- and Career-Changing Decision	9
3 Balancing Home and Work	15
4 Real Change Isn't Easy	19
5 Six Keys to Leading an Effective Change Initiative	25
6 Making Decisions That Stick	31
7 Dealing with Really Difficult Issues	39
8 How to Get Teachers Who Say No, to Say Yes	45
9 How May I Contact You? Let Me Reduce the Ways	53
10 Only Hire Superstars	61
11 Enhance Your Reputation—Make Every Meeting Matter	71
12 What Your Office Tells Others About You	79
13 Playing the Visibility Game	83
14 The Kiss of Death	87
15 If You Allow It, You Approve It	93
16 Parents Are Your Best Friends	97
17 How to Become a Savvy Principal	105
About the Author	115

Preface

The majority of my professional life has been spent working in schools as a principal, teaching in graduate programs preparing principals for licensure, or working in the field coaching principals. Even though I have not been a "real" principal for many years, I still think of myself as a principal, as do the principals I work with on a daily basis. I know the role inside and out, backward and forward. I am, by all accounts, a principal at heart and practice.

As an unabashed advocate for outstanding principals, my work has focused on providing all principals with the opportunity to succeed. I believe most principals have the desire to be great; they just lack the critical insights and knowledge to be so. They just haven't learned yet how to become savvy.

I was the principal of a school that received a number of awards including being recognized as a National School of Excellence. I have worked with principals in all venues and at all levels: large city schools, small rural schools, affluent schools, high-poverty schools, schools where forty-three languages are spoken, and schools where English is the only language. In the past ten years, I have worked with principals and staffs in schools identified as low performing that became high performing in two to five years.

What I have done in each situation is become a skilled observer of principal behavior. For over forty years, I have watched principals who have led significant successful change efforts in their schools. I have examined and reflected on what these leaders have done that average or less successful principals have not.

My experience has taught me that savvy principals do things very differently from the average or less successful principals and what they do differently will never be found in research studies on effective school leadership. These individuals see leadership from a perspective more unique than that of leaders in average or low-performing schools. What are the beliefs, behaviors, and attitudes of these streetwise and savvy principals that are not uncovered in the research but that these savvy principals know make a difference?

What I have discovered is that no one has written about principal leadership from this unique vantage point, and there may be logical explanations for this. For instance, most studies on principal leadership tend to replicate or tweak previous research, and this is not your typical quantitative study. Another and probably more feasible explanation is that no one has studied the behavior of principals from this unique view because researchers are asking the wrong questions. In other instances, principals are reluctant to put their comments in writing because of their controversial nature.

Or, if they have this knowledge, they are not writing about it. For example, in university life, unless every written statement made by the author is supported by some other academician's work, it is not considered academic. As such it is not considered scholarly and does not count in academic circles.

Over the years, I have been sharing what I have observed with students in a graduate seminar on leadership. The focus of the class is to help students learn what specifically to do the first couple of years on the job so they don't get fired. The class also addresses those behaviors that will make principals excel often and early in their positions.

Students have come to appreciate the uniqueness and simplicity of the information. A frequent comment from students about what I share is that it just makes sense. They ask why more principals don't do these things and why there aren't texts that share these insights. It is with their strong encouragement that I write this book.

Who is the book written for, what is my voice, and how do you go about reading this book? My audience is the harried graduate student studying to be a principal and the overworked, yet aspiring, individual who is one. It is also applicable to other leaders in schools and businesses that are looking to improve their performance.

Realizing that the busy administrator or graduate student does not have the time to read long chapters in lengthy books, I have written the chapters in a concise, engaging, and light manner. If I could make my point in one paragraph with five to seven sentences, instead of two lengthy paragraphs, I did. (I am indebted to this publisher for allowing me to emphasize brevity, as most textbooks are priced based on the length of the manuscript.)

You will find no references to research studies or academicians in the narrative. This book is about only what I have observed, reflected upon, and drawn conclusions from. In other instances, the lack of citation is the result of not knowing whom to give credit for the idea. I have changed the names of people mentioned and have not listed accurately the name of any school.

Authentic personal stories create the stage for the insights I share. I was personally involved with each story while as a principal, an observer, or a coach. I want each story to engage readers into asking themselves what they could do or how they could use this information.

This book is unusual in its organization. Except for the first chapter, which should be read first, you can read the book in any order. If a chapter title sounds interesting, read it. Each chapter provides guidance and strategies for doing the job more effectively in a shorter amount of time and with increased wisdom. Equally important are those chapters focusing on what not to do and what critical mistakes to avoid.

And, finally, I am always interested in hearing about the adventures of savvy principals. Please contact me if you have any questions or wish to engage in further dialogue about the book. I hope you find my voice engaging, the book enjoyable, and the information career enhancing.

You can reach me at jcapelu1@maine.rr.com.

Introduction

This book is about how you become a savvy principal. Savvy principals do things very differently from other principals. What they do that distinguishes them from others will never be found in studies on effective leadership building. There are two reasons for this: (1) researchers are asking the wrong questions, and (2) even if researchers were asking the right questions, principals would be reluctant to put their responses to those questions in writing because of their controversial nature.

It is well documented that the current role of school leader is more demanding and difficult than at any other time because of pressures from national mandates, extreme special interest groups, and increased calls for more accountability. Yet, it is also well documented that the role of principal continues to be the single most important variable to student learning and school success. In those schools that are deemed as "doing well," leaders think and behave differently than leaders do in low-performing schools.

What are the beliefs, behaviors, and attitudes that are not uncovered in the research but that savvy principals know? This book provides you with specific and candid strategies for how to become a standout leader. It tells you how you should act and behave as well as how to positively influence others' behavior so you can be successful. Because, in reality, if you are successful, students will be successful, teachers will be successful, the school will be successful, and the superintendent will be successful. If this is the case, then it naturally follows that the school board, parents, and community will be proud and happy about what is happening at their school. Everybody wins if you come out on top.

So what is a savvy principal? It is someone who pays equal attention to each of eight critical aspects of their role. As important as these areas are, it is the clear and well-delineated focus on these eight dimensions that sets these principals apart. Although they are described in no particular order, you can't implement these aspects in a piecemeal format, nor can you do seven of eight and think you are a B+ administrator.

It's all or nothing to be a savvy principal. The eight aspects are vision, leadership, organization, culture/climate, program leadership and direction, school–community relations, professional growth, and balanced wellness.

VISION

Savvy principals have an overall vision of the school and its programs which is consistent with the vision of the school district. This skill is specifically related to their ability to frame and articulate to staff, colleagues, and the community short- and long-range goals. The vision drives all the work of the school. Without a clear focus, the school wanders from one new idea to the next, without meaning, connections, or closure. If no one knows where she or he is headed, then no one can take any satisfaction in getting there. This focus must be laser like. All great schools have a clearly framed and articulated plan that is known to all.

LEADERSHIP

Savvy principals make their leadership permeate all operations of the school. This includes the capacity to encourage, assist, and enable colleagues, staff members, and students to excel. It assumes the ability to get others involved in groups to solve problems, interact with a group effectively, and through collaboration lead them to completion of a task. To lead the group effectively, principals must be highly skilled as facilitators and problem solvers themselves. When appropriate, this means making decisive, unilateral decisions that are in the best interest of all constituents.

ORGANIZATION

Savvy principals are able to skillfully and efficiently manage the routine and technical aspects of the job. This generally includes such things as tending to the day-to-day operations of the school, managing the business aspects, transmitting information and policy to staff, producing reports that are accurate and timely, and managing records and internal accounts. In general, it is the ability to identify, plan for, and effectively and efficiently use the resources available. They make optimum and selective use of the latest technology to support this work. More important, they work hard to make the mundane fun.

Introduction

CULTURE/CLIMATE

A key role of savvy principals is in establishing expectations, which are closely related to establishing a positive working and learning climate within the school. In general, this means that there are high expectations for student and staff behavior and achievement. It means that a commitment to excellence is maintained within an environment that is conducive to learning. There are a number of other characteristics of a positive climate, which include such things as the expectations for teachers' success in classrooms, a feeling that open lines of communication exist within the entire school community, and a sense of positive feelings toward achievement by students and teachers. Developing a learning environment that is open and accepting of different beliefs and perspectives is paramount to a healthy culture.

PROGRAM LEADERSHIP AND DIRECTION

Savvy principals continually demonstrate an understanding of teaching behaviors associated with classroom learning. They know what great teaching is, and they are relentless in their expectations that great teaching should be the goal of everyone who works with students. In addition, it is expected that the processes of instruction and student learning will be monitored on a regular basis and evaluated by the principal. Principals are in classrooms engaging in conversations about the curriculum. They ask questions such as what important content will our students need to know in ten years and how is the information they are expected to learn relevant to the students when they are learning it. In general, evidence of school leadership will result in coherence within the instructional program and an ongoing dialogue about the future.

SCHOOL–COMMUNITY RELATIONS

Savvy principals attend to the development of productive relationships with various segments of the community and help establish strong, positive, and open lines of communication with parents. The principal seeks the active involvement of parents and community members in the meaningful work of the school through serving on committees, volunteering in classes, and mentoring students. The leader effectively communicates the school's expectations to the community at large and, when it is appropriate, seeks the engagement and support of external organizations to assist in the implementation of school goals. For example, the principal may collaborate with local businesses to ensure that those students working in their businesses during nonschool hours are attending school and doing well in their studies.

PROFESSIONAL GROWTH

Savvy principals are expected to be the number one role model for lifelong learning in the schools. It is assumed they will participate in school and systemwide committees, workshops, and conferences; maintain memberships and involvements in professional organizations; show receptiveness to new ideas and change; and encourage staff to acquire new knowledge. If you are not learning, you are regressing. You can't stay at status quo. Savvy principals are always learning in an effort to be smarter and more effective in their role.

BALANCED WELLNESS

To be effective leaders, savvy principals recognize that they must maintain a healthy lifestyle. To be able to perform under pressure and in situations of conflict, leaders must develop and implement strategies to maintain their own well-being. In addition, they must learn to balance their work commitments with their responsibilities at home. Without this balance and attention to their physical and mental well-being, leaders will not be able to be outstanding performers at work.

No one ever said being a principal was an easy job. The responsibilities can at times be overwhelming, and often you have to deal with issues you never imagined. If your school has a strong set of core beliefs that are public and well known, then you must be the gatekeeper of those values. All decisions should be based on whether they are consistent with those explicit values. Students, staff, and community members should expect and demand that their leaders be vigilant in the overseeing of those values. Being consistent means not sending mixed messages.

People may not always agree with your decisions. In fact they won't, but they will respect your decisions if your frame of reference is clear and known to all. Although a majority of the decisions you make will be gray, there are some that will be clearly black and white. For leaders to be great, their positions on critical matters must be crystal clear. The voice from the principal's office has to be strong and emphatic.

In summary, savvy principals see themselves as active participants in the schools. They are philosophically committed to change and innovation. They are confident in what they believe and can articulate those beliefs to others. People do not have to guess what is important to them. They will take a position on an issue even though it may be unpopular. Savvy principals do not sit in their offices as the world goes by and blame others for the problems that exist.

Savvy principals are not content with the status quo and see problems as opportunities. They encourage exploration and risk taking. When roadblocks occur, they remove them or assist staff in discovering ways around them. They diminish the burden of organizational constraints on the work of the school.

They understand that working in schools is hard, and they seek ways to encourage, not discourage, efforts. They don't always play by conventional rules. They do not feel the need to take credit for the success of the school, but rather, they enjoy it when all parties get recognized. They are not afraid of losing their jobs because they know they can get another one.

So how do you become a savvy leader?

Acknowledgments

I want to thank all the streetwise and savvy principals I have worked with over the years. The opportunity to collaborate with and learn from them has provided me with much of the context and content of this book. Many of the stories mentioned are about them, although the names are different. These are special leaders who are smart. They know how to get things accomplished in a manner that is thoughtful and deliberate, and they display a high degree of integrity. In particular, I would like to acknowledge the exceptional leadership skills of Camille Barr, Rick DiMillio, Judy Eberson, Tom Edwards, Ted Finn, Dick Klain, Rob Leibow, Bob Lyman, Mike McCarthy, Scott McFarland, Valjean Olenn, Roger Shaw, JoAnne Sizemore, Barbara Tague, Cherie White, and the late Terry Despres and Ken Nye.

And many thanks to the graduate students who reviewed the chapters and provided terrific feedback. Since we require graduate students to take risks in formulating and expressing their ideas, I thought it would be a unique opportunity for them to see how a professor does likewise when conceptualizing and writing a book. The process became a wonderful and rich dialogue about what constitutes effective leadership and how one becomes a streetwise and savvy principal. I would especially like to extend my appreciation to graduate students Greg Applestein, Andrew Lupien, Drew Patin, and Laurie Rule for the extra time they committed and their thoughtful perspectives.

I would like to thank Jolene Spence and Jennifer Rock, both terrific graduate assistants, who provided meaningful feedback on the substance and technical aspects of the manuscript. Appreciation also goes to Kathie Bickford, my administrative assistance, for her support.

I would be remiss if I did not thank my family for their help. My wife, Vanessa, provided critical wisdom and constant support throughout. The perspectives and insights she provided as a master teacher and valued colleague helped me to refine and hone my thinking. My daughter, Jill, a dynamic young teacher, assisted me with technical aspects of the manuscript. She also helped me rethink some of my ideas as a result of conversations we had about leadership.

My son, Andrew, currently an undergraduate at Emory University, shared examples of effective and ineffective leader behavior he observed from his role on university-wide committees. These conversations assisted in sharpening my focus. In addition, I would like to thank my sister Judy, who serves as a mentor to new teachers, for her unique perspectives and insights on many of the topics.

In the late 1980s, I met Tom Koerner when he was the editor at the National Association of Secondary School Principals (NASSP). I proposed to him the idea of writing a monograph about middle-level education that would serve as a resource for principals who wanted to learn more about middle-level education but did not have time to read a lengthy book. From that collaboration, *Middle Level Programs, Practices and Policies* was published.

Nearly twenty-five years later, I contacted Tom and presented my ideas for this book. I shared with him my vision for writing what I had learned during my career about what effective principals did that made them unique and special. I am grateful to Tom for his knowledge and remarkable ability to take complex issues and frame them in a manner that is easy for authors to understand.

I would like to thank Carlie Wall, Emily Natsios, and Erin Cler for their enthusiastic and friendly commitment to detail in the preparation of this manuscript.

And, finally, my gratitude to all the principals who work diligently in the field each day to make schools places where students and staff can be successful.

Chapter One

Selecting the Right Boss and Community

Being successful as a principal has as much to do with having the right boss as it does with your level of competence—maybe more. It is much the same with being a student. If students have great teachers, they learn more. Great classroom teachers create an environment in which learning is structured, engaging, challenging, and fun. They encourage their students to take risks, want them to succeed, remove barriers that may impede their learning, and take responsibility if they don't succeed by trying other teaching strategies.

Great classroom teachers understand there may be outside issues that sometimes get in the way of their students doing well each day in school, and they provide encouragement instead of punishment for that. They hold high expectations for their students to do well and give direct, constructive feedback with the intent of improving their performance. They are confident in what they do and see their role as vital to their students doing well. If students perform well, then teachers perform well.

All of this is true of great bosses. They believe you can do the job and see themselves as partners in your success. They strongly believe that if you succeed they succeed. They understand the difficulties of your position to be challenges rather than obstacles to your success. They provide clear expectations for what you are to accomplish and offer frequent, constructive feedback on how you are meeting those standards. They make sure you have the necessary resources, both human and financial, to support what you are doing with staff and students to enhance the learning of both.

Great bosses make sure you and your staff have opportunities to continue to learn and grow on the job. They don't micromanage your building, but they do provide a buffer between you and the school board members. They understand you have a personal life outside work and respect the time you spend with family and friends away from the office. They believe that for you to be effective you must maintain a healthy lifestyle, and they willingly provide resources and support for that to happen.

So how do you go about finding that great boss? Initially, you begin by doing significant research on the community you are considering to get a sense of its past history and future possibilities. It is critical that you learn as much as you can about the community before you apply. If it's not a fit, do not waste your time or theirs. All jobs are not great jobs. Much of the information you need to obtain can be gleaned from community, school, or state web pages. Here are some research guidelines:

With respect to the community, compile the following demographics:

- Location, type of community, and historical development
- Current per capita income (or some other measure of "wealth") compared to the state average. (Is it a wealthy, poor, or middle-class community? What is the median household income and percentage of people below the poverty level?)
- Types of housing: percentage of rental units and owner-occupied dwellings
- The population in 1970, 1980, 1990, 2000, 2010, and currently. (Are there trends? Is it a growing, stable, or declining community?)
- The percentage of school-age children compared to the total population in 1970, 1980, 1990, 2000, and 2010
- Social characteristics (Is it an affluent, a blue collar, a bedroom, or an agricultural/rural community?)
- Educational attainment levels of the population

With respect to the schools, compile the following:

- School enrollments in 1970, 1980, 1990, 2000, 2010, and currently. (Are they going up, down, or staying the same? What are the future enrollment projections?)
- Elementary school per-pupil expenditures compared to state average
- Middle school per-pupil expenditures compared to state average
- Secondary per-pupil expenditures compared to state average
- School organization (How many schools are there, and what are the grade level configurations of each school?)
- Active parent–school groups (Do they exist and what do they do?)
- Dropout rates for the past five years
- Graduation rates for the past five years
- Number of students receiving free or reduced lunches
- Number of ELL students

- Number of middle, elementary, and high school principals in the past ten years
- Number of superintendents in the past ten years
- First step on the teachers' salary scale
- Highest step on the teachers' salary scale
- Number of teachers with master's degrees or higher
- Staff and teacher transient rates
- Student transient rate

With respect to the governmental structure, look at:

- Type of municipal government
- Type of school district (single municipality, consolidated, multicity, or township)
- Size and composition of school board
- Tenure of present superintendent of schools (career or place oriented)
- Tenure of present town/city manager or equivalent official (career or place oriented)

With respect to the political/social nature, look at:

- How the school board functions (dominated, factional, pluralistic, or inert)
- Recent "hot" issues in the community
- What groups/individuals hold political power
- What strategies the school leaders/advocates use to secure educational support and resources

Compiling and analyzing this data provides a detailed community profile. It allows you to determine whether this may be a community you would feel comfortable in and enjoy being a member of. You should also have a clear understanding and knowledge of what it takes to be successful there.

As a bonus, if you decide to apply for the position, you may, in fact, know more about the schools and community than some of the people who are interviewing you. This knowledge is guaranteed to impress the committee because it demonstrates that you have done your homework and gives the appearance that you are sincerely interested in the position.

People who serve on interview teams are usually deeply committed to the school and their community. They will be especially pleased that you cared enough about their school and them to really do extensive homework. Therefore, it is logical to assume that members of the interview team might project you to be a leader who will always take the time to thoughtfully consider the implications of your actions before you act. This is a good thing for you as a candidate.

Let me be clear. There is no model community where your success is a given. Being successful is broadly defined. Certainly, if you choose to work in an affluent, well-educated community with mostly expensive single-family homes, few if any tenement houses, little or no free or reduced lunch population, no homeless shelters, and low transient rates, you may not have to worry about how students will perform on standardized test scores. However, there are certain to be other issues.

The critical point is that there must be symmetry between your beliefs and what the community values regarding what is educationally important. If the two are not congruent, you cannot be a standout leader in this particular community. Look for another community where there is congruency in values.

Once you have found a community with which you match values, you want to closely scrutinize the person who would be your boss. What information do you need to determine whether she or he has the potential to be the great boss you need to become a standout principal? How do you go about getting that data? You can conduct some of this investigation by searching online. What is written about the community, schools, and school boards? Check to see whether they have a Facebook or web page. Do they have a blog or Twitter account on the school system website? Many people will post their résumés on LinkedIn. What can you glean about them through what they have written or what has been written about them?

So what do you really need to know about your prospective boss? Here are six key questions you absolutely need to have answered:

1. *What positions have they held prior to this one?* Have they been teachers or principals and done jobs similar to the one you are applying for? Were they successful in previous administrative positions? Did they go a nontraditional route to their current jobs, possibly having been a bank executive or hardware store manager? Do they have any graduate training in school/district leadership? Will they understand the nuances of what you do and how different the public service sector is from private business? Will they know and understand the issues and challenges that come with your position?

2. *Is this their first superintendency?* If it is, you need to analyze this situation very deliberately. It could be a career-threatening or career-enhancing situation. Let's talk about this in more detail. As with any first job, there is a steep learning curve. They may be so consumed in trying to learn how to be successful in their job that they won't be able to give you the time and support you need. If the superintendent has to choose between spending time on his or her efforts and helping you, whom do you think he or she will select? If the superintendent says he

or she would like to help you but doesn't have the time, don't apply. You are not a top priority.

The second option is that it could be a great opportunity. If you determine this person is highly ambitious and wants to use this job as a stepping-stone to better opportunities, then this can be a terrific opportunity. In reality, superintendents look impressive only if individual schools are successful, and all the schools in the system don't have to be high-performing schools to do this.

Many a superintendent has hitched his or her wagon to one school in a district and used that publicity to garner another more prestigious position. In this instance, each school and the superintendent recognizes that one's success is directly tied to the others. If, however, they are willing to support you philosophically and provide the necessary resources needed to lead significant change, this is good. In this scenario, you might want to seriously consider applying.

3. *Do they look healthy or out of shape?* Why is this a key question? If they do not value taking care of themselves, then what priority do you think they place on making sure those who work for them lead healthy lifestyles? Probably little or none is the correct answer. They may not understand the importance of taking time to eat lunch or exercise. There is always a slight chance that although they don't value wellness for themselves they do value it for others. Take time to explore what wellness options are available for administrators and staff.

4. *What do they have for outside interests?* Most individuals who are successful have an interesting life outside work. Work should not be their entire life. Time away from the job lets one have fun, rejuvenate, and enjoy family and friends. If they have no outside interests, it is a safe assumption they will not value your time away from the office. As a consequence, they will expect you to work too many hours and always be available (24/7) to answer their questions or respond to a constituent. They will not respect the boundaries between work and home. Sometimes individuals work the number of hours they do because they don't want to go home. Work becomes that excuse. This is sad. Remember: in a high-stress leadership role, you can work only so many hours a day and be successful. At some point, you just get yourself in more trouble when fatigue and resentment enter the day.

5. *What professional organizations are they contributing members of?* If they are actively involved at the regional, state, or national level, then they probably are committed to the advancement of the profession. What educational initiatives do they write or speak about? If they want to influence policy agendas, this can only pay dividends to your district. This is a good thing because it means they will probably expect you to become involved with those organizations appropriate to your

role. Savvy leaders are extensively involved with state and professional organizations, which serve to improve their craft knowledge and provide access to like-minded principals. If they are participants at the policy level, it can mean more funding and resources for you because they will have access to that knowledge before others do.

6. *How do they promote their own professional development?* Do they attend school-system workshops and state and national conferences on a regular basis? What are they interested in learning more about? You could also check to see what the system's financial commitment is to staff development. What are the policies on travel and conferences? Are professional development monies included as part of administrative contracts? Remember, what is valued gets funded. Again, if they are interested in upgrading their own knowledge base, then they will expect you to do so also.

7. *Do the principals respect and like the superintendent?* This may be a tough one to glean, as you may have to be careful with regard to collecting data. On one hand, the superintendent may be a high-profile individual and have a reputation that is well known to all so that most people agree one way or the other about him or her. On the flip side, the superintendent may keep a low profile, which would require that you carefully dig around for some clues. Assume that everyone you speak with is on the interview team—nothing is confidential. You might begin by asking people why they like working in the district.

    Check to see what the principal and staff turnover rates are. If the superintendent has worked there for an extended period of time and principals come and go on a regular basis, that is probably not a good thing. If principals state that the superintendent is a "good person and great to work for," that is a plus. Probe further and ask why. You could check to see what the superintendent's relationship is with the school board. Is the superintendent in control and valued, or does the board micromanage the district and potentially your school?

8. *Check other resources and documents.* Look at district documents to see whether there is a vision and strategic plan that is recent. Does the superintendent develop an annual state of the district report, complete with goals and data, to chart system and school progress? Checking with colleagues you went to graduate school with is another excellent source for this information. You can also visit some of the local stores and ask people what they think about the schools. Calling area real estate brokers and asking for communities with great schools is another excellent source. Reading the local newspapers can also offer glimpses into community perceptions or the superintendent's relationship with the press. If you become seriously interested in the position, get as much information as possible.

Getting a balanced perspective on the overall competence and quality of the superintendent is sometimes hard to ascertain. With the anti-administration attitude that seems to permeate our country today and the easy access to technology to express one's views, usually without filters, very few school leaders escape criticism by someone or some group. By doing the necessary homework, you should be able to get a fairly good idea of the person who may become your next boss. Combining these questions with the community profile will help give you a fairly accurate picture of the school and your prospective boss.

Remember, you are always a free agent, seeking the best opportunity to utilize your expertise to better yourself and the community you serve. Every job opening does not have the potential to be a great job. If you do your homework, you greatly maximize the chances of finding the terrific opportunity you are seeking. Savvy principals always do their homework even before they know exactly what their next assignment is going to be.

Chapter Two

Where You Choose to Live Is a Life- and Career-Changing Decision

Jo Anne had been warned. Administrative colleagues had told her that returning to her hometown to be the new middle school principal had more liabilities than assets. She had heard all the horror stories of what had happened to others, but she was sure it would be different for her. After all, she had been valedictorian of her class, star athlete, and model student citizen.

Everyone was proud of the fact that she had attended a prestigious New England college and graduated with honors. She had gone on to get her master's degree and doctorate, taught for several years, and been a very successful middle school principal in a metropolitan area.

She was now returning with her husband to her small-town roots to raise their two children. Her spouse was an author whose occupation allowed him to live anywhere. Her family was well respected in the community. Her parents owned two car dealerships. It was the perfect scenario, so she thought.

Her hiring was viewed as a wonderful happening in the community. The school had experienced some shaky leadership the past few years. The previous two principals did not relocate to the community when employed. It seemed that having one of their own assume the helm was welcomed by all. At first, everyone congratulated her on being the new principal and coming back home. They envisioned she could be a role model for students. They were optimistic that she would be able to turn the school around.

Before her return, there had been a lack of discipline at the school, and test scores were below where they needed to be. The state had deemed it to be a failing school, and that was not acceptable to this proud community. Morale was low. Someone needed to steer the school in the right direction. Most community members agreed she was the one to do it.

When she arrived at school, she had a small plaque made for her desk with "Dr. Jo Anne LeClair" printed on it. All the stationery had to be redone to read "Dr. Jo Anne LeClair," embossed near the top. She hoped it would serve as a role model to encourage students to strive to achieve advanced degrees. The secretary had to call her Dr. LeClair even though they knew each other growing up. She did this because she thought it would bring needed respect to the position. She could tell that her secretary was uncomfortable with this formality. She also asked the teachers to address her as Dr. LeClair.

During the first week, she had to suspend a student for using inappropriate language directed toward a staff member. He was a junior and key player on the soccer team. In addition, he happened to be her neighbor's son. She knew it was the only thing she could do, as she could not show favoritism because he was a neighbor's son. If she did, she knew she would lose the respect of the teachers. If she got the reputation that she treated students differently because of who their parents were, she knew she was dead.

Because of the suspension, he did not play in a game that afternoon, and the team lost. She could hear the undercurrents at the game. It was uncomfortable, but she knew she had done the right thing. She was not sure one player could make that big a difference, even if he was the goalie.

It was more uncomfortable the next day at breakfast when her daughter asked her why she had to suspend Molly's brother from school and the soccer team. Molly was good friends with her daughter, and the two spent a lot of time at Molly's house. Jo Anne's daughter told her that Molly felt the team lost because of Jo Anne's decision. Jo Anne's daughter asked if that was true. Jo Anne did not have a good explanation for her. Because of confidentiality reasons, she could not talk about it. She found it hard not to be able to explain to her daughter what had happened.

It got worse when she attended a neighborhood get-together that weekend. It was obvious her neighbor was not happy with her son's being suspended and was avoiding her. Others also seemed to be a little distant. She felt very uncomfortable making small talk. For the first time, she questioned coming back to the community where she was raised, to work.

The boy returned to the team, and the season ended well. The team made the tournament and advanced as far as predicted. The suspension turned out not to be a catastrophe.

For the next few months, things seemed to go well. It was nice living so close to the school. She enjoyed being able to go home for dinner if there was an event at the school that evening. When she went into stores, people were again telling her they were glad she had come back to the community. She was getting along with her administrative colleagues and liked the collaboration that was evident with the leadership team.

At the end of the first semester, she had to confront a teacher on a potential disciplinary matter. A parent had sent her an e-mail that accused this teacher of telling her daughter that if the new restructuring plans were implemented her parents should consider having her attend another school next year. Because of its failing school status, the school was required to make significant changes to how it was organized and how it delivered instruction to students.

This teacher had been vocal in her opposition to these changes. Although recently the outward comments had deceased, it appeared that she was still not supportive of what was going to take place. This was going to be an even more difficult conversation because they were friends from high school and had played sports together. She realized that it would be a lot easier situation to deal with if this were not the case.

The meeting with the teacher did not go well. At first, the teacher denied making any such statements, saying she was insulted that Jo Anne would even think she would do that. After all, they had known each other for a long time. Jo Anne indicated she was not taking sides at this time, but because of her position she would have to interview the student and other students in the class to find out what happened. If the teacher did not make those comments, she was sure that would come out.

Jo Anne knew she could not take sides without additional information. That would not be good for the teacher or her. When confronted with the parent's e-mail and the possibility of having to defend her action to the student's family, the teacher admitted she might have intimated the comment. She then went on to say that many people did not like having to call her Dr. LeClair and that she must have forgotten where she had come from. Since they were friends, could Jo Anne show her support for the teachers and side with her?

During the conversation, the teacher added that this parent was too involved with her daughter's education and always tried to make the public schools look bad. By making such a big deal of this, the parent was looking for another chance to do this. She also said the last principal supported teachers and he was not one of them. Jo Anne told the teacher she could not ignore the concern of the parent by stopping the process at this point.

Jo Anne shared with me that this was not a pleasant situation and she did not enjoy having to deal with it. There was a lot at stake here. Her credibility with parents, her friendship with the teacher, and her ability to be seen as a leader who was impartial were at stake. Jo Anne began to realize that this was not an issue in the previous systems she had worked because she knew no one prior to being hired.

Her husband had also noticed that when they went out to dinner or shopped at the grocery store people wanted to talk to her about something school related. These seemingly harmless exchanges could last five to thirty minutes. It seemed to him that she was always at work. There was never a time, even at home, that she was not working. People would still call or stop to talk if they were out in the yard.

Her husband noticed that people seemed to pay close attention to what they purchased for alcoholic beverages. She and her husband did enjoy a glass of wine while dining out or entertaining friends in their home. They agreed that it would be better to not have a drink while eating at a restaurant in town. What if they had one glass of wine at a restaurant and someone who had an axe to grind accused her of driving after drinking? How could she be a role model if she was doing that?

They also decided they would buy their alcoholic beverages and recycle their returnable bottles in another community. This seemed to be getting ridiculous. She did not have a drinking problem, but they were starting to act like she did. This job was starting to dramatically impact their lifestyle in a negative way.

At the end of the year, the elementary school her children attended held a recognition ceremony. It was a time when students were acknowledged for their learning achievements and citizenship behavior during a well-attended, traditional community celebration. At this event, both of Jo Anne's children received two of the most prestigious awards, and she and her husband were extremely proud.

They worked very hard to be good parents by trying to teach their children the right things to do. They were proud that their children were recognized for being "good citizens." The next day at dinner, her children told her that kids at school were saying the only reason they won those awards was because she was the middle school principal. The other kids did not think they deserved them. They asked if that were true.

Later that evening, Jo Anne admitted to her husband that it was a mistake to have moved back to her hometown. Although she loved being the principal in her hometown, it was a mistake to think that she and others could separate her personal life from her professional life. It was having too great an impact on the whole family.

The only advantage she could see from being a principal in her hometown was a shorter commute. Although her husband mostly had been silent on the issue, he now wholeheartedly agreed. They both seemed relieved.

A year later, Jo Anne took a principal position in a community twenty-five miles from her hometown. They bought a home in a neighboring community, and things worked out much better. Life was as normal as it could be for a school administrator.

Whether to live where you work has always been a topic of much debate. Some people seem to be able to do this with little consequence. They weave their personal and professional lives seamlessly within the community. They like being the principal, and connect their identity to that role. It is important to find balance between home and work. Wherever you choose to live, remember that it is not just about you. The impact on your family deserves equal consideration.

Postscript/full disclosure: I never lived in the cities and towns where I worked as a public school administrator. When I began my career in administration, there was pressure to live where you worked. I would get asked in interviews whether I would move to the community if offered the position. I think there were several reasons for this question. Some board members viewed it as a commitment to your job. How could you commute and fulfill the responsibilities of the role?

Some considered it to be a commitment to the community. If you lived there, you were more likely to be involved in community activities, for example, church, recreational, and civic activities. Some also felt that if you were going to be paid by local dollars you should spend your money locally. That meant paying local property taxes and buying locally.

Although I never lived in any of the communities I worked in, I never once missed a meeting or school event or left early because of my commute. When people asked me when I was going to move closer, I would reply that it was not financially possible for me to do that at that time. That seemed to satisfy most people. Not once did a school committee member ask me how much the school needed to raise my pay so I could make the move. I always worked as many hours as I needed to get the job done; no one ever questioned my commitment.

In each position I held, the commute was about forty-five minutes one way. I actually found that very helpful. In the morning, I used the time to get my thoughts together before arriving at work. I could think through issues I knew were ahead of me, use my voice recorder to record ideas I had for projects or thoughts for letters I needed to write, or get caught up on the local news on the radio.

The time riding home was by far the more beneficial. If I had had a tough day, it allowed me to unwind and debrief before greeting family members. Most times, I had worked through the stress of the day by the time I got home and did not take it out on family. If my commute was only a few minutes, I'm not sure how I would have handled it.

Also, when I was home, I was not at work. I did not see students I had just suspended, parents who were upset with a teacher and wanted to talk to me about it, or teachers who were unhappy with a decision I had made regarding their teaching schedules. Nor did I have to share family time with those who wanted my work time. In my neighborhood, I was not the principal of the local school but a neighbor. I was like everyone else. I liked that I was not special or the center of attention. And so did my family.

Chapter Three

Balancing Home and Work

A huge problem almost all new administrators confront is figuring out how much time they need to spend to be successful at work. Most feel they have to work longer days than anyone else in the building to let others know that they are committed to the job. They want to project the attitude that they will do whatever it takes to get things done. That may include getting to work before everyone else and being the last one to leave.

Add to this dilemma the fact that there are usually expectations from the superintendent, school committee, staff, students, and parents that you need to "work until the job is done," but rarely is "until the job is done" defined.

When is the job done? The real answer is never, but new administrators do not know that yet. The one constant is that all the constituencies listed above want the principals to be there for them when they need them.

Teachers like to see principals in the hallways and cafeteria. Students like to see them wandering around the school and in classrooms checking to see if things are safe. Parents and students alike enjoy seeing them at school events such as plays, art festivals, and sporting events. The superintendent and school board like to see them at all of the above. Causing additional tension is the fact that their spouses/significant others and children like to see them at home.

It is easy to lose perspective trying to be all things to all people all the time. This need often results in novice administrators working too hard and too many hours. I often see the stress on the faces of principals as they try to rationalize to me why they had to miss their child's dance recital or soccer match so they could attend a curriculum meeting.

Recently, one principal shared with me his wife's displeasure with his missing so many family get-togethers on weekends. The sad part was he hadn't realized he had missed so many of them until it was explained to him.

The wife thoughtfully went through all of the gatherings, one by one, that he had missed. Even sadder are those that never realize it until it is too late.

I vividly remember being a new principal and feeling the time pressures. Luckily, an event early on in my career shaped my perspective on how much time I needed to work and how I could be successful without sacrificing family and friends. Let me explain.

I was invited to a three-day conference on how to make the principalship more attractive. Back then, as with today, the job was seen as difficult and time consuming. At the conference were other principals who were new like me and veterans who were about to retire. Although we had stimulating dialogue, in all honesty we did not accomplish much in those three days. It was nice to spend time at an ocean resort free from most of the pressures at work and to meet new people.

However, I was not lost at sea for three days. I ended up taking away from that conference something that profoundly changed the way I would look at the principalship. What was that event?

On the last day of the conference, we were all asked to share our reflections of what we had learned and were taking away from our experience. As we went around the room, each one took a turn. Frankly, most of what the participants said you would normally expect to hear at sessions such as this, for example, the usual comments that it was great and a rewarding use of time. I knew some of the people and that they were distorting what they had told me earlier. We were all polite and paying full attention.

Then it was Alex's turn. Alex would be retiring that year. He was a well-respected veteran of a large secondary school. He had been state principal of the year as well as president of the state principal's association. His comments were brief and powerful.

He said, "This has been a difficult conference for me. I have come to realize in these three days that I have raised everyone else's children but my own. I cannot undo that, but you new administrators can." We all admired him for his candor but also felt deeply sorry for him. He had given his life's work so that others could profit at the expense of his family.

I tell that story often to make an impression on new administrators. One time, after I shared this story with a group of aspiring administrators, a woman came up to me and said, "I know whom you are talking about. I think the person you are describing is my father-in-law, and you are absolutely correct."

Given unrealistic time demands, perceived and actual, what is a principal to do? Here are three suggestions on how to balance your work hours with family and outside life:

1. *Before you take any job, ask the superintendents what they do for fun outside school.* If they say nothing or that the job is their life, don't

work there. If they say that it is an expectation held by parents to see them at every event, don't work there. Do not accept a position that will not work for you. If they mention they have a variety of interests they pursue on weekends and vacations, this sounds promising. If they have a life outside school, they will probably not begrudge your having one either.

2. *Never learn the security code of the building.* Every district has one person who has the responsibility to oversee the buildings and associated problems. Usually, they are given a truck to ride around in and deliver materials. Most of the time, they are locals living in town. If you learn the code, some will expect you to go to the school every time an alarm goes off. You probably aren't going to be the first one in the building anyway. The police and fire department personnel will be there. They are getting paid to work weekends—you aren't. Let them do their jobs protecting the safety of individuals and property. This is another strong reason for living out of town.

3. *At the outset, establish that weekends are for your family.* Tell people what you will be doing. On Mondays, talk about what you did. If someone questions your whereabouts, you can say "With this job I don't get to see my kids, wife, or parents, etc., as often as I would like. I did not want to miss another game, family party, etc. It is hard to explain to my children why I can watch other kids all the time but have no time to spend with them." One principal I know, every Sunday, sends his staff an e-mail that includes a review of what happened at school the previous week and information about key events that will take place in the upcoming week. He starts each review by talking about what he has done with his wife and daughters, be it a trip to the mall, a softball game, or family time. He always mentions how important that time is to him and hopes that they have done the same with their friends and family members.

You can work only so many hours a day or week and be effective. The pressure of the position does not allow for many breaks during the day. Drawing a line between work and home offers the best possibility for you to be successful at both. If you are forced to choose, always choose home. If you are a savvy principal, you can get another job in which you will be appreciated and your time and what you bring to the system valued.

Chapter Four

Real Change Isn't Easy

There are a zillion books written by experts that provide wonderful guidance on how to lead change initiatives in schools and organizations. A recent web search using the words *change in education* and *change in business* uncovered four thousand books currently available. They tell you assumptions about change, rationale for change, strategies for change, steps to follow for change, pitfalls for change, and so on.

Some authors claim that if you follow their six or twelve, or whatever number, of easy steps, you too can be a successful change agent. Upon close examination, you will find that leadership voyeurs write many of these how-to books on school change. They have never actually led an initiative, but they have on occasion observed it or conducted interviews with actual school leaders who have. They glean their expertise as observers, not real participants.

Don't you love that term *change agent*? Some even use case studies or examples of schools and businesses that have changed, to substantiate their positions. In many instances, you are led to believe that it is not that difficult. If you read their books carefully, you will have the knowledge to be successful. Wrong!

Substantial change is difficult work and can be a major career enhancer or ender. That is why in reality it is so infrequently undertaken. Most school leaders just work around the edges of change or just tinker with it a little. It is more about smoke and mirrors than substance. Leaders add a program here and there to look good and take pressure off themselves from those who want something done. The goal is to look like major changes are taking place, when not much is really happening.

The purpose of these initiatives is usually program specific in nature. These initiatives are highly visible and identifiable. You want the initiatives to have an identity, but to have the changes impact only a few students or staff in the building. If you can get a small core of staff to go along with what you are proposing, you can usually make it work. Examples would be freshman teams or academies at the high school level, an interdisciplinary team at the middle that loops, and a multiage team at the elementary level.

All of these options usually offer choice to parents and students, while giving others the choice to opt out. Program options also allow those faculty who wish to participate the opportunity to do so, while not forcing less enthusiastic staff to be part of the change initiative. You hope that the venture will be so successful that there will be an outcry from all the nonparticipants—staff, students, and parents alike—to be included. You hope they will even be insulted that they were not included earlier.

Never say you are going to pilot a program. Pilot programs are a bad idea. They sound like experimentation—that you have no idea what you are doing. They imply that you are the first principal in your community, first in the state, first in the country, first in the world for that matter, to be doing this work. Therefore, it is of such magnitude and high risk that you must pilot it, like you did with your dissertation research or a chemist does in the lab with a group of cancer patients and subsequent control group when introducing a new cancer drug.

Unless you are undertaking an initiative no other educator in the world has ever tried, don't use the word *pilot*. Most Americans may also confuse pilots with TV series, and as we all know most TV pilots go nowhere. Why would you ever try something that was not grounded in previous work and had some basis for your beginning the work that you are proposing?

How do you go about doing this? First of all, and most critical, the work that you are about to undertake must be important to the students and school. It has to be identified as an issue that needs time and attention to be addressed. In most cases, it would be a new initiative with several possible options for action. You cannot begin unless you have some data to suggest it is an area that needs immediate attention.

For example, if 60 percent of all freshmen flunk one or more classes during their first semester of high school, it would seem to be an area to be addressed. This is clearly not what you would like, but it may not matter if they all go on to graduate. It can be dismissed by staff as just an unintended and natural consequence of making the adjustment to the rigors of high school. If this is the case, you are stuck with the "it is not a good thing but not serious enough in the long run to convince us to do something different" attitude that most principals face from staff when proposing a change in the way school is constructed and conducted.

But if you can couple that data with other data that show that, of the 60 percent who fail one or more classes the first semester of their freshman year, 30 percent fail to graduate within four years, then you may be on to something. It is not you who are proposing a change in practice for whatever reason, but rather you have some verifiable information to suggest there may be a serious issue that needs addressing.

What is important is that you don't own the issue. You are not doing this because it is an area you want to address. It is not your issue or an agenda you are trying to promote. It is a school issue that everyone owns. You want to remove your identification as far as you can from the "why" issue. The why should not be you. The why has nothing to do with you. The why has to do with a student need, not your need.

This is a critical piece in having an initiative succeed. It cannot be about the leader, or the initiative will usually fail and the leader will become a short termer. You are not the reason for the change; the issue is the reason for the change. That has to be perfectly clear and understood by all at the outset and throughout the process. It is the most critical piece of learning in this entire chapter. If you stopped reading this chapter here, you would be halfway to being a successful "change agent."

Nothing is ever really new or truly innovative in education. Every change builds on the previous work of others. The same is true in all professions. In medical research, what is often proclaimed as a major discovery is built on the many years of others' work. In education, an initiative may appear to be new, but in reality it isn't. It may just be new to you.

Your next step would be to examine what has happened in the past in the school and the district surrounding this issue. You must diligently do your homework. Involve others in this process to build interest and ownership. The earlier in the process you do this, the more likely the endeavor will be successful. This can't be *your* endeavor. Ask these questions:

1. Have there been earlier attempts to deal with the issue, and what have been the results of such efforts? How has this recently become an issue that needs attention?
2. Are there any current political or cultural concerns that impact the success of this project?
3. What is the school's or district's commitment to the issue in terms of educational and financial support?

Let's examine each of these questions in a little more detail and use as a point of reference the dismal freshman data on failing classes. Your first action is to check around to see what the past history of freshman success has been. Ask the guidance department what long-term and recent data are available about this issue. Have they regularly kept and reported this information? If so, have these figures been available, and who has known about this information? Have these figures been kept quiet by the administration, and if so, why do they perceive that to be the case?

In some schools, there is a culture that all perceived "bad news" is kept under wraps, so to speak. The principal or other leaders, including the superintendent, do not want certain information made public on their watch.

An obvious example of this to most people would be building maintenance. In most districts, long-term maintenance programs are not well planned or are sporadic. In tight budget times, if there is an aging boiler or roof that may need repair, it is usually not listed for funding or is cut from the budget to save staff positions or programs.

Superintendents and board members know that it would be rare for parents, teachers, or students to lobby the school board to save the roof or replace the boiler. They are more likely to attend numerous board meetings to save freshman football or middle school band than to replace an aging roof before it leaks. Administrators are not dumb.

Roof or boiler booster groups would be an extreme rarity. Nor are state or national conferences for principals filled with sessions on how to deal with roof and boiler booster groups. The topic does not make many graduate syllabi. There is a reason for this.

Also contributing to this lack of action on issues is an underground code that prohibits any public criticism of what happens or doesn't happen in the buildings. In some schools, there is a quiet, unhealthy, underground culture of benign neglect that exists between the staff and administrator.

A key assumption that lies underneath this bond is the unwritten and unspoken assumption that if you don't tell on me as a teacher, I won't tell how bad you are as a leader. If you will let me do what I want in the classroom, I won't say bad things about you to students and parents or in the community. Your role is to defend me to the students and parents. Defend usually means support and protect.

If we agree to this code, then we can peacefully coexist in the school. Maintaining the status quo becomes the norm. Any attempts to do otherwise threaten the balance of power and will result in winners and losers. In almost all cases, the leader is the loser. The teachers in the building usually last longer than most leaders do, and they know that.

Now, back to the issue. If it is not a new issue, what attempts in the past were made to deal with it and how successful were they? Getting this information should not prove difficult. You may be able to get this data from staff or the central office. There may even still be staff members at the school that were part of these efforts. Find out in each attempt what the specific needs being addressed were, who the targeted students were, who was involved, how it worked out, and what data are available.

In most instances, you will probably find that little data are available and that most peoples' recollections are not positive. The reason this is true is because, if it had been successful, those practices would still probably be in place. What you will learn from this inquiry will be invaluable to ensuring that the next attempt you are involved with will have a great chance to succeed. You do not want to repeat past mistakes. That is why it is crucial for you to do your research.

If you do your investigation as your first step, you can identify those areas that were issues and address them. You will appear very smart by doing this. Part of your strategy is to avoid repeating previous mistakes. Staff members are tired of failed initiatives that seem to be repeated, with little or no consideration being given to past botched attempts. Don't make that same mistake, or you will suffer the same fate. The scope and scale of the initiative determines the short-term consequences for you.

It is a more serious and long-lasting problem for students who cannot get that time and opportunity back. And that is the reason anyway for any change initiative—to make the learning situation better for students.

Now turn your attention to the political/cultural arena. Is there pressure to increase graduation rates? Has your building been identified as a low-performing school either by the state or when compared to other schools in your district? Is there a certain demographic within your school population that is not achieving at a satisfactory level? How public are those data? Are these new issues or are they ongoing? If they are new, how were they identified? What is the will of the community to act?

If all the data and supporting evidence indicate that there is support for addressing the identified issue, what are the next steps? If something makes sense, then you should be able to convince others that it makes sense. You will have identified a need, done your homework by looking at what others have done, and then built support in the school and community to do this work in your school.

Is there a will to do this work on the part of teachers and administrators? Does the community actually want the change to occur that is needed, and will they provide the necessary financial support? Real, substantive change is never cheap. If the initiative calls for the formation of a study group and time to do that work, it needs to be funded. If it calls for visitations to other districts to see what others have done prior to implementation, that needs to be funded. If it calls for new learning on the part of staff, then it is imperative that funds be allocated to cover the costs. If it calls for additional materials or staff, that needs to be funded also.

Many times districts will timidly admit there is a need to change but find excuses not to do it, the primary one being the lack of dedicated funds to make it happen. If they do not fund it, what they are really saying is that it is not a priority at this time. Other needs come before this one. The rhetoric does not match the reality. If you have no money, you have no support.

Don't begin something that you cannot follow through on. That is much worse than not beginning at all. For any change initiative to be successful, the foundation for success must be there. Any savvy principal will tell you that.

Chapter Five

Six Keys to Leading an Effective Change Initiative

To be recognized as a successful principal, you need to do something significant. To do something that gets everyone's attention, you need to change something that is not working and make it work significantly better.

Some changes are easy to initiate and do not require significant effort. You can improve involvement in schools by parents and community members by increasing the number and types of activities that allow them to be engaged in the life of the school. For example, you can start a principal's advisory group or hold monthly senior citizens' luncheons at the school. You can do this without having to involve many people, and hence, need little commitment by staff members, the superintendent, or the school board officials to make this happen.

These are highly visible change initiatives that in the short term gain much needed positive publicity but in the long term may have little impact on the quality of teaching and learning at the school if that is all that is done. Streetwise and savvy principals know that these moves are important and effective tactics only as part of a well-thought-out game plan not done in isolation from the overall strategy.

When we think about a significant change initiative today, we most often think of having to improve test scores in a school that has been labeled as failing. This school identification is usually made as the result of a demographic group(s) not doing well on a portion(s) of some standardized testing measurement. To change this situation requires a number of purposeful, broad-scale commitments from various stakeholder groups such as students, teachers, administrators, and the community, as well as the will and knowledge to do so.

Recently, I have worked as a consultant/coach to principals in two school systems, both identified as low-performing schools. One was a middle school and one a high school. In both schools, significant gains were made in test data within two to four years. I also have knowledge of schools that were also identified as failing but that did not make successful gains over the same time period. There are some distinct discrepancies in what those schools that made significant gains did differently from those schools that did not. In fact, in several instances and over several years, scores actually declined and remained there. What are those differences?

It should be noted that real systemic school change is a complicated undertaking that requires a thoughtful and articulate effort, one that requires all pieces of the plan/strategy to be implemented simultaneously.

The first key to successfully making dramatic changes in the school is that the justification for the changes cannot be your idea. There must be various sources of data that unequivocally point to the sense of urgency of doing business differently. You cannot be the one to identify the problems and then propose solutions. You need to be seen as the leader of the change initiative, not the identifier of the need. The principal can, however, play a crucial role in identifying strategies to address the need.

The second key is that the mandate to change is strongly supported by the board of education. Simply speaking, there were no split votes by the policy body on whether to go forward. This is a critical piece because it sends a clear and convincing message to staff that this work is to be taken seriously. If staff members see any gap in this support, it can tend to empower those not enthused about the new work to undermine the leadership of the principal.

It gives them confidence to garner support from like-minded resisters by referring to a fragmented board. Their thinking is, if we can raise questions about the changes proposed, we have a sympathetic ear from parents and the community. If we are effective in influencing these individuals, we will not have to do anything differently.

It is also critical that, throughout the change efforts, when there are difficult and at times controversial decisions to be made, that the board continues to act as one voice. There can be no holes in the armor. Any opening can be seen as questioning the recommendations of the leaders. This will spell disaster. In those schools that were successful in making changes, strong board support occurred throughout.

Another key is that the superintendent is a participant in the process and an unwavering advocate for the principal and staff. The superintendent is the lead person in the change initiative. She or he is the one who from the outset works with the board and community to build support for the work that needs to be undertaken. This is not an easy task. Most communities find it hard to accept the fact that their school might not be performing at a level that an outside group finds acceptable.

For all the concerns we read about in the press about how poorly our public schools are doing, most people think those descriptions refer to other communities. Most are very proud of where they live and do not like hearing unflattering things being said about their schools. They take those comments personally. I have consulted with schools that chose not to accept financial help for just this reason. They took the approach that no one is going to tell them that they have a failing school in their community and they do not need any money to get better.

The superintendent needs to convince the community, through the use of data and persuasion, that this is an opportunity rather than a punishment. How can we use this opportunity to increase the staff's knowledge to make the learning better for students is the key focus question. Where schools have succeeded in making significant gains, the superintendent was prominently involved in influencing the community, but let the principal play the leading role in the school. The superintendent was never seen as the quasi-principal but was there to support and encourage the principal throughout.

The fourth key was that all schools that showed significant growth had plans that guided their work. The length and detail of the plan was not a factor, as the documents varied in length from six to fifty-eight pages. The critical components were that they were based on the needs identified, had reasonable strategies, were well thought out, involved stakeholders in the development, and were reviewed and updated on an ongoing basis.

The plans were not just pieces of paper that were placed on shelves. They were guiding frameworks to focus the enormous work being undertaken. It was a visible demonstration of the beliefs and values of the district. It answered the questions What are we going to do? How are we going to do it? And how will we know if we have done it?

The fifth key is to act fast and reassess often. Most schools tend to make changes only at the beginning of each school year. If a problem is discovered in November, no changes are usually made until next August to correct it. If a program, for example, is not working and not going to right itself without some form of intervention, then why not make some changes at that time? What benefit is there to waiting?

Here's an example. At one high school, it was learned in March that approximately fifteen of the 150 in the senior class were in danger of not graduating. Upon further analysis, it was determined that it was possible, with some extra help and willingness on the part of the students, that they could make it.

The school decided to start an after-school program called Food For Thought. It would be a two-hour tutoring lab, one day a week, followed at the end by dinner. Four teachers were given stipends to run the program. It was also deemed that the program should be open to all students in the school. Selected students were encouraged to attend by staff. The program grew in numbers from an initial cohort of ten to twelve to forty. As graduation neared, there were still seven students who would not make it across the stage.

The school reassessed where these seven students were and determined that with more time and willingness on the students' part they could complete all the work by the middle of July. Since their state compiles graduation rates July 31, the school determined to have a second graduation in July for those who completed all their requirements. All seven students completed their work, a graduation ceremony was held with parents and grandparents, and these students can always say they graduated with their class. The graduation rate was 100 percent.

How many do you think would have enrolled as fifth-year seniors or completed their diploma through adult education? If the past were a predictor of the future, not many would have graduated. This is just one example of how important it is to act fast and use data to make decisions and reassess often. It is not that difficult; it just calls for a different perspective.

The fifth key is to, at the outset, spend time and money on those ready and willing to follow the game plan. As principal, you need to get out of the gate quickly and establish credibility for the course of action. Therefore, it is important not to spend too much time trying to convince those who are reluctant to change. The expectation is that all will change, but we know how difficult that can be. Although doing school differently is an option, just saying or mandating it does not make it a reality.

Time, attention, and resources should be given to those staff members who are seen as credible with other staff members and respected within the community. It is those individuals whose opinions carry weight with other staff and members of the public. If these staff see the benefits of early efforts, it is more likely others will join in or at least not attempt to derail progress. They can aid in the plan gaining momentum.

Time spent trying to convince staff who are lagging or resisting diverts energy and is not a good use of your time initially. This doesn't mean that they don't need to be involved. Make decisions based on what is in the best interest of your top teachers, as long as everyone is held accountable.

There are some who probably will not change their beliefs. Those staff may choose to leave, or they may not. If they stay, it is imperative that you hold them accountable for their behavior. You are not concerned with what they believe, only how they behave.

The sixth key is to communicate and publicize what you are doing on a regular basis. It is imperative that all the work being done at the school is as widely shared as possible both within the school and the community. Marketing is an area that schools, by and large, do not excel at.

There will be many misgivings and much misinformation spread by those opposed to the substantive changes taking place. This is usually done in hopes that they won't have to do anything differently. It can be a very effective strategy if left unchecked.

Keeping all constituents informed is not only smart, it is a necessity. Getting as much press coverage as you can about the positive happenings is a great morale booster for those doing the hard work.

As a principal, never, ever take credit, or appear to take credit, for anything good that happens at the school. Remember that any success that occurs is always the result of the hard work and effort of staff, students, and parents. If the staff members ever get a hint that you want the credit for the accomplishments, they will stop trying and gradually stop supporting you.

You want to be at the photo shoots, but you don't want to be in the photos. The less you are quoted and the more staff members are quoted, the more ownership they will seek. Making significant improvements at the school is not about you advancing your career, even though it really is. It is about creating an organization where students and staff can optimally learn and grow together by developing structures and opportunities that will be sustained after you leave.

You have to be aggressive in seeking venues to promote your school. Think of it as the school going through the process of rebranding or as though you are opening a charter school and need to compete for students. How would you go about doing that?

Be proud of the work that is being done by staff and students. Provide them with venues to let their good work be known by others. In the end, everyone will get the credit they deserve, including you.

Chapter Six

Making Decisions That Stick

Being consistent with how you make decisions is a hallmark behavior of savvy principals. The number of decisions principals have to make daily or the level of seriousness of those decisions rarely overwhelm standout leaders. Whether deciding how to handle a parent who has a complaint about a teacher or explaining to the student council president why seniors are in danger of losing their privileges, or figuring out whether to change the school schedule because of a special assembly, savvy leaders follow a similar process each time they decide what to do.

What you are aiming to accomplish is a consistency of methodology. Do you have a consistent process that you follow when confronted with having to make a decision: a low- or high-stakes one? Savvy principals do. Mediocre and poor leaders are reactionary in nature and do not follow any thoughtful and consistent way of going about making decisions. They treat each incident as separate, making it difficult for those around them to get a sense of what they will do or why they did what they did. They are unpredictable.

Being consistent does not mean doing the same thing in every situation. It means following the same logical process in each situation to arrive at what your course of action will be. The outcome of that decision is not always apparent or universally acted on. With all the decisions you have to make daily, it is impossible and illogical to think that everyone will agree with every decision you make. New principals dream about this happening, as they usually want everyone to like them. But in reality that is not possible or even desirable.

Over time, people will usually forget what you decided, but they will rarely forget how you went about it. If they cannot figure out the protocol/strategy you employed to arrive at the decision, they will wonder what criteria or process you actually used. It is in these instances that your credibility as a leader is questioned. The doubts about your competence to lead can result in numerous questions, which are not good for you if you want to be taken seriously.

People may wonder whether you made the decision you did because you were pressured by someone. Did you like someone better? Was he or she a friend of yours or the friend of a friend? Did you bother to take the necessary time to get all the facts before you acted? Were you biased by former dealings with the individual(s)? Did you not see this as important? Did you not understand the far-reaching implications of your actions? Do you have any core values that form the basis for your actions, or do you take the path of least conflict/pain for yourself?

Of all the doubts people could raise, this is the most severe. When people say they are not sure of what you stand for, they are actually stating that you really believe in nothing of substance. You will change positions on issues as it best serves you, not the school. You will in fact stand on a fence so wide it is impossible to fall off. This does not inspire others to have confidence in your ability to lead a school through difficult times.

So what do standout leaders do differently? They act in a manner that is reflective, impartial, and inclusive, and with integrity. They ask themselves eight questions when confronted with most decisions. The questions are listed below and followed by examples:

1. What is the specific scenario?
2. What additional information is needed before any action can be taken?
3. What is the primary issue(s) to be addressed?
4. What action will you take?
5. Who will benefit from your actions?
6. What opportunity does this situation provide for you to strengthen your ability to lead?
7. How will you know it is the right decision?
8. What did you learn?

Let's take an example that is fairly common. A parent sends an e-mail to you regarding a complaint about a teacher. The e-mail reads something like this:

> Dear Principal X,
> I am sending you this e-mail to express concern over a grade my son received in Mr. Finn's AP American History class. The grade is totally unjustified. I contacted Mr. Finn to find out why my son received a B+ and was told that it was because of class participation. He said that if the grade in this area had been higher he would have received an A. With this grade, my son will not get high honors this semester. It is the first time in his three years at your school that this has happened. I want you to change the grade immediately so his chances of getting into X college are not harmed. I talked to my neighbor who

is on the school committee, and she said you could do this. He is a great kid, and this is very upsetting to him. Please let me know when I can view this grade change online.
Respectfully,
Ms. Z.

Just below that e-mail is one from Mr. Marcotte, the teacher, who is new to your building.

> Dear Tom,
> I wanted to make you aware of a complaint I received from Ms. Z. She is concerned her son did not get an A in AP American History and wants me to change the grade. Part of the grade is determined by class participation, and his grade this semester for this area was not very strong. He does not deserve an A. If you want more information, I would be glad to meet with you. I appreciate your support in this matter.
> Thanks,
> Bill M.

As you are reading this e-mail, you get a call from the superintendent. He tells you the chair of the school board has called him because a friend of hers is upset about an unfair grade. The superintendent wants you to take care of the matter in a way that causes as little fanfare as possible. He tells you to do what you need to do to keep this under the radar. There are some delicate teacher–board contract talks going on, and he does not want anything to get in the way of those. He also reminds you that the administrators do not have a new contract yet and keeping the board chair on our side will be important. He is fully confident that you know how to resolve this issue to the benefit of all parties. He urges you to make this a priority. He hangs up.

Your secretary overhears the conversation and tells you that the parent who is complaining is a pain in the rump. Because her family owns several businesses in the community and has donated substantial money to renovate the football stadium, she feels entitled to preferential treatment. She goes on to tell you that the woman has a well-earned reputation as being someone you don't want to cross and as a result most teachers give her children preferential treatment. It is just the way it is and everyone knows it. She also tells you that a board member just called and wants you to call her back. She thinks it is about the grading issue.

Let's go through each question.

WHAT IS THE SPECIFIC SCENARIO?

What do you know from the information you currently have? In short, a parent has complained about what she feels is an unjustified grade that her child received. She appears to be an individual used to getting what she wants, but you don't know that firsthand. The teacher feels the grade is justified. The superintendent has received a call from the board chair about the situation, and he wants you to resolve the matter immediately, to make the chair happy and probably him, too. A board member has called to speak to you, and you assume it is about the grade.

WHAT ADDITIONAL INFORMATION IS NEEDED BEFORE YOU TAKE ANY ACTION? WHERE DO YOU START?

Standout leaders know that the more information they have about a situation, the better decision they will make. If you fail to get the needed background data, you usually end up having to retrace your steps at some point. Not taking the necessary time to do your homework increases the likelihood that you will screw up. It is better to take the extra time to get as much info as you can to save you time in the future reexamining the issue because you were lacking some key pieces of data. Because if you mess up, it is really never over with. So with those parameters in mind, what do you need to find out?

Some information is easy to obtain but time consuming. In this case, some background data might be found in the student handbook, while some you would need to gather by talking with individuals. You need to learn whether there are general schoolwide grading policies and, more specifically, whether these policies are of such detail as to include class participation.

If they do include class participation as a component, do they spell out what percentage of the grade makes up class participation and, more importantly, how class participation is defined? Also, is there a rubric for class participation and if there is, how is that communicated to students? If it turns out there is no schoolwide standard, is there a department policy for grading that includes class participation? If the answer is again no, then you have to hope that the teacher has created a clear definition of class participation with an associated rubric and communicated that to the students.

You will also need to look at the teachers' contract to see what is required if you receive a complaint regarding a teacher. Most contracts specify that if a complaint is made regarding a teacher by a parent that the teacher must be notified promptly. That means you must tell him or her. You have no choice and that is a good thing.

Contracts usually state, and justifiably so, that teachers must also be told who the complainant is. This is also a good thing. The accused should know who the accuser is. This is the same right you would expect if the superintendent informed you that there was a complaint against you. The rule to adhere to is that whatever the protocol is, you follow it. You never want to be seen as a leader who is lax in adhering to contractual agreements. You always want to be viewed as a leader who respects employee rights, including your own.

Although this is a delicate issue, you need to find out what the protocols are in the district for board members contacting principals directly. Is it an accepted practice that the superintendent allows? If not, are there one or two board members who ignore that procedure and contact principals when they feel like it under the guise that they are responding to their constituents? Or is this a very unusual behavior because of some personal interest a board member has with this situation?

WHAT ARE THE PRIMARY ISSUES TO BE ADDRESSED?

There are several key issues involved in this scenario. What are the grading policies at the school, and have those been made public? Do students know what they need to do to succeed? Are there systems in place that would allow students to know how they are doing throughout the semester so there are no surprises at the end of the term? Was the grade justifiable? Are there protocols in place for school board members to interact with principals? Is it the norm that school board members call principals directly without going through the superintendent?

Another key issue is what the protocols are for dealing with parent concerns about teacher behavior, and are they being followed? Is there a clear process in place that allows the issue to be resolved at the lowest level? What is the student's role in resolving the grading issue? What attempts has he made and how has that been handled?

WHAT WILL YOU DO?

One of the first things you would do is to acknowledge the e-mail. Tell the parent that you were not aware of the issue. If there are protocols to be followed, then include what those are. Tell the parent that the process must be followed and that if after doing so the matter is unresolved to her son's satisfaction that you will become involved at that time. Tell her to please let you know how it works out.

It is to be hoped that this will take care of the situation, and that is the end of your involvement. You then call the superintendent and tell him the situation has been resolved. If that proves not to be the case, which sounds likely, and she contacts you again, tell her you need to gather information and will be back in touch with her within a given (be specific) time period.

You would also call the superintendent and apprise him of what is happening and what you propose to do. It is at this point that he needs to support your plan for resolving this issue. If he cannot do this, ask what he would suggest. At this point, you would need to talk to the teacher to get the specific details of the grade.

Begin by asking the teacher a simple question: If the student and parent appealed the grade all the way to the school committee, do you have justification for the grade? Can you show evidence that the criteria for a grade, including all the components that constitute the grade in this class, are clear? For example, is it spelled out how much homework, quizzes, tests, class participation, and other areas count toward the final grade? Do you have a definition of class participation? Does the student know what he needs to do to get an A in class participation?

Regardless of the outcome of this meeting, you will need to meet with the student to get his understanding of the issue. How does he feel about the grade, and what explanations can he provide? In these situations, it is appropriate to have another adult present, usually another administrator or a guidance counselor.

It may be that a meeting with the teacher, student, and yourself is the most logical next step to resolve this matter. If that does not occur or if it does not work out, then a meeting with the parent is in order. This meeting would include all the vested parties. It is to be hoped that this meeting would resolve the issue.

To find out what the rules are for board members contacting principals directly, you could check with another principal, or you could go directly to the superintendent. Or you could do both, which is probably the best choice.

What opportunity does this situation provide for you to enhance your ability to lead? As a new principal, this is a great opportunity for you to establish your credibility as a leader. You want to be seen as someone who gathers information before taking any action, solicits input from those affected by the situation, uses a logical process for arriving at decisions, and has the best interests of the students and staff at the forefront.

It is also a great opportunity to begin a discussion schoolwide on grading practices. You can frame this around the need to be clear and consistent throughout the building. Teachers need to see that it is not only in the best interest of students but also in their best interest to have thoughtful consistency. In reality, that may be the only reason for them to act.

For what it is worth, you are not as concerned with the motivation for this action but rather the results of this action. If you are able to get agreed-upon grading standards, then you will get clearer expectations for student performance. When this occurs, everyone benefits, students and teachers alike.

This situation also gives you a chance to clarify with the superintendent how you are to respond when contacted by a board member. If he states that it is accepted practice for board members to contact you directly, then don't unpack your boxes. Principals cannot be effective if their bosses cannot manage the behavior of board members. You need to have only one boss and that must be the superintendent.

WHO WILL BENEFIT FROM YOUR ACTIONS?

If this situation is handled correctly, everyone will benefit. The student will receive a grade that is justified, the teacher will have made clear what his expectations are, the parent will be satisfied that a fair process has been followed, and you will benefit from being perceived as a person of reason and integrity who wants what is best for students, teachers, and parents. The superintendent will be happy because the chair of the school committee is off his back. He also knows that he made a good hire. In summary, if you handle this correctly, you will benefit the most. Your ability to lead will be enhanced.

HOW WILL YOU KNOW IT IS THE RIGHT DECISION?

The primary indicator is that the student receives a grade that is justifiable. He may or not be happy with the grade, but he will understand why he received the grade. He will see it as fair. There will be no fuzzy math. If it is not a grade he wanted, he will learn what he needs to do to get that grade. Secondary indicators might be the student, teacher, or parent thanking you for how you went about handling the issue such that there were no perceived winners or losers. If one or more of them do that, this is good. This might not happen immediately, or it might not happen at all. Finally, and most important, you will know that you made a good decision, and with that self-knowledge you will be ready for the next dilemma.

WHAT DID YOU LEARN?

You learned what the role of board members is in the day-to-day operations of the school. You learned how strong your new boss is. You learned about whether there are grading policies in the building that are clear and consistent and make sense. You got a glimpse into how people responded to the decision-making process you wish to implement.

Being a savvy leader is all about making one great decision after another or helping others do likewise. To do that requires a process that is thoughtful, respectful of the needs of everyone, and consistent in nature. Just as we want to teach students to make responsible choices, be they intellectual or personal, so too do we desire the adults in the building to do likewise.

Savvy principals model those strategies in their daily work. Dysfunctional principals do not. As a principal, you clearly make the choice of the type of leader you want to be. In the end, it is not a multiple-choice question. In this situation, unlike most others in schools, there is only one right answer. The process you use for making difficult decisions has to be clear, thoughtful, and consistent. You receive no partial credit as principal for getting it somewhat right. You have to get it right every time.

Chapter Seven

Dealing with Really Difficult Issues

If you watch divers at swim meets, you understand that there are various degrees of difficulty associated with each dive. These levels are determined by how hard and sometimes how dangerous the dive is. Obviously, the more risk and skill involved, the greater the potential of scoring more points. If you take the safe dives, you can still win the meet if someone who chooses a more difficult level fails. Although scoring is a complex system that takes into account a number of factors, at the end of the meet, the individual with the most points is declared the winner.

At times, the work of the principal can be compared to that of a competitive diver. Principals make many important decisions and become involved in situations each day that do not usually result in physical injuries, nor do they, if handled properly, become career enders. Thankfully, the horrific school shootings, although too many in number, have not become commonplace. Handling a call from an irate parent concerned about her son's grade in math, dealing with a teacher who is fed up with a student's behavior and wants that student out of her class, or negotiating with the transportation director over a bus incident make up the bulk of the daily pressures for any principal. For skilled leaders, these issues are mostly routine in nature. Over time, they develop protocols/strategies they use to mediate these differences. They know what the agendas are of each group and follow a logical path to a resolution of differences, one that is usually agreeable to all. Most situations they handle are private matters and do not involve a larger audience. Even if conflicts do not work out to the complete satisfaction of all the parties involved, not many other people know about them. Like the diver who chooses the safe dive, these situations are low risk but have a potential for a high reward. The interested parties can see the principal as a fair, ethical person.

There are other difficult issues principals confront that ratchet up the stakes, those having the potential to severely limit their future capacity to succeed and, in some instances, lead to job loss. In these situations, the actions or inactions of principals are as important (and at times maybe more so) than the outcomes.

For instance, the principal's integrity may be compromised to such a degree that he or she loses his or her credibility. For example, he may yield to the unrealistic demands of a special interest group or show preference to the child of a school board member. In doing so, he loses the respect of the teachers and is rendered incapacitated. He now has the reputation of being able to be influenced by certain power groups. Now when he speaks, no one really listens.

Staff may decide that the principal doesn't have the will or capacity to stand up for what she really believes. Or she may have lost the support of the superintendent, as evidenced by the lack of backing on tough matters. As a result of this loss of integrity, staff members begin to individually act on their own without consideration for the group. They also tend at this point to rapidly move into "bunker mentality." Bunker mentality is when the staff members ask themselves what they need to do to survive until the next administrator arrives. The principal is leader in title only. She has been reduced to being a figurehead. She has power only by that granted through the organization, namely position power. And a veteran principal knows that if she has to rely solely on the authority granted to her by her position title, she is ineffective.

There are defining moments in the principal's work that mark his future. These are occasions when how he handles a controversial issue will determine whether he survives. Unfortunately, there is no predicting when these moments may occur, no clear warning signs. So in reality, you need to operate each day in a manner that prepares you for those moments. Let's talk about one of those situations and how the principal made the right decisions.

This career-ending scenario deals with the actions of a very popular teacher who used somewhat controversial teaching practices. This particular teacher could be very sarcastic and condescending to students who were not doing outstanding work in his class. At times, he would publicly embarrass them by chiding them in class for not completing homework. He would say things such as "You must be working four jobs. That is why you can't get your homework completed."

He also would frequently tell inappropriate jokes that were gender and race biased. He had attended a highly respected college and never failed to remind students and parents of that fact. He also would reference his college to make fun of other teachers who went to so-called less prestigious universities: "What did Mr. Daley [another teacher] get on his SATs? The answer 'drool.' Or how do you get a [local college] graduate off your porch? Pay him the pizza delivery money."

Before he made these remarks, he would say to students, "If you have a problem with anything I say, please speak to me. If you go to the administration first, they will just ask if you have spoken to me." This continued for many years. Some students were afraid to say anything in case it would hurt their grades; some unfortunately laughed, and others did not know what to do because they were afraid of the control and power this teacher possessed.

This teacher took these same teaching strategies to the head coaching position he held at the high school. What parents saw was a group of athletes who were able to win state championships. What they did not see, except for infrequent outbursts at games, was the verbal abuse he used to get the kids to excel. During practices, he would yell and scream at players. If he did that during a game, some parents saw it as a very effective communication strategy, unless it was directed at their child.

Parents did not know what happened in the classroom, but it could be rationalized on the field as acceptable to occasionally embarrass and humiliate kids in public because the main goal was winning. It was referred to as discipline, motivation, and accountability.

If an athlete dared to complain, the implied threat was that he would not play. Many of his athletes were also recruited to play in college, some at the Division I level. Players thought that they needed the coach to speak favorably to college coaches if they were to have a chance at competing at the next level.

To make matters worse, if two players' skills were somewhat equal, the coach gave preference to the student whose parents held more political power. He was a strong advocate for his program, many times at the expense of other sports/activities. He would often tell his players that for them to have a chance to play in college they needed to focus on one sport. At times, this caused issues with his coaching colleagues as well as with some parents.

As a result of his behavior and a parent willing to come forward with damaging classroom information, the superintendent suspended him for two months. To make matters more controversial, this happened during the middle of the season he was coaching. The decision was not made without considerable reflection and consultation, but it came as a shock to most. The response by some students and community members was quick, loud, and angry.

Many felt the teacher was suspended not for his abusive behavior toward his students, of which most were unaware, but rather because the principal was upset with him for daring to challenge his style of leadership. Others viewed it as a classic power struggle between two strong-willed individuals. They felt the principal wanted to be in charge of everything and did not want anyone to challenge his authority. Still others thought the principal was jealous of all the publicity the teacher received through coaching awards. Whatever people believed, it was a decision that had the potential to divide the school and community.

Some students immediately scheduled a meeting with the principal to express their concerns. They did not know why the teacher was not allowed to teach or coach but saw it as unfair. They liked him as a teacher and also were concerned they would not have a chance to win another championship without him. The students did not understand the reason the teacher was suspended and why the principal could not tell them the reason.

After the meeting with the principal, they seemed to be more agitated. Later in the day, the principal was informed by a reliable source that the students were organizing a walkout the next day after lunch. He had heard from allies in the community that parents were helping the students get organized. It seemed that Facebook pages and Twitter accounts were abuzz and texting rampant over the issue.

The principal knew that if the students walked out he would have to suspend them. For some students, this would mean they would be unable to compete on the team of the suspended coach. For other students, it could impact their grades. Some administrators and teachers thought that threats would stop such action, but he wasn't convinced this would happen.

He was also within the legitimacy of the position to suspend the students. There was the strong possibility that that strategy might backfire, causing more protests and unwanted attention toward the school and him. It would also not change the fact that some students and parents were upset.

He wondered how he could fend off the uprising while maintaining his status as an emerging leader. He knew that the school board, central office, parents, students, and staff would be closely monitoring how he handled this situation.

After some rather quick reflection with his assistant principal and the athletic director, he decided to call a meeting of the school leadership council to discuss the situation. Instead of seeing this situation as a huge problem, which it was, he looked at it as an opportunity. Having students suspended for walking out would not solve the problem.

After consulting with the council, he decided to use the situation as a teachable moment on how to show students how to protest legally. They quickly determined which teachers and administrators would be best to do that and organized a schedule to make it happen. They also enlisted the services of two attorneys who had children at the high school. The history teachers quickly put together a civics lesson on how to legally exercise your rights. The next day, the teachers, the two lawyers, and the principal spoke to students in smaller venues.

The lessons went well, and the students gained knowledge that all responsible citizens need to know. The students were grappling with an issue that was current and relevant to them. They could immediately apply what they had learned. The walkout did not occur.

This process did not make the anger and questions go away. Some people were still perplexed over why this teacher was suspended and made their opinions known in the school and community. Not many minds were changed. What did occur was the fact that the situation did not escalate to a point where innocent people were hurt.

No one was suspended or had his or her grades impacted. No threats were made, and no one was challenged to act. What could have been an explosive situation was not only defused, but significant learning took place.

A critical role of the principal is to establish a positive, constructive learning and working environment within the school. Part of this means that discipline is maintained within an environment that is welcoming and tolerant of differing perspectives. The key viewpoint the principal took in this instance was to see this possible nightmare as an opportunity rather than as a problem.

A belief that problems are horrific and must be done away with as soon as possible is not only unhealthy, it is debilitating to leadership. In this sort of environment, people look to blame others for any dilemmas that arise, and risk taking becomes nonexistent. A productive environment cannot flourish in an organization where ownership of problems becomes singular.

Savvy principals see problems, even those with the potential to be job ending, as opportunities. To do otherwise doesn't make the decision less fatal; it merely becomes a question of how soon. Savvy principals know their integrity is tested daily. And these leaders know that their integrity can never be taken from them, only given away by themselves. Savvy principals never take a leadership position they are afraid to lose.

Chapter Eight

How to Get Teachers Who Say No, to Say Yes

A surprise to most new administrators is that there are staff members who behave badly. As a teacher, you knew there were a few colleagues who whined and complained, but you generally didn't have to deal with them, and most of the time their actions did not directly impact your work or success. On occasion, you may have heard a disparaging comment in the staff room about having to implement another initiative or a sarcastic comment about one of their students who they feel should not be there, but generally if it did not directly impact you, you probably ignored it. Rather, you spent most of the day in your domain, hung out with teachers with similar beliefs, and were rarely influenced by their abhorrent behavior.

As an administrator, you do not have this luxury. You cannot simply choose to avoid these individuals, because their bad behavior does impact you and everyone else. You have to deal with it.

Most new administrators are ill prepared to challenge individuals who are defiant and difficult. Having to confront difficult staff members is not a pleasant experience for any administrator, beginning or seasoned. Most individuals assume the role of principal hoping everyone will like them. Most principals enjoy people and want to be liked in return. Education is a people business, and we all want everyone to get along.

Most of us don't seek conflict in our professional lives. However, there comes a time for principals when avoiding conflict at work causes more problems for them than dealing with the issue. In many instances, avoiding conflict causes more conflict.

One illustration is the principals who selfishly place students with challenging behavior issues with the best teachers in their schools. They know that they won't have to deal with the students with discipline issues that will be sent to the office or their parents who will complain, and rightly so, that their children are not succeeding in their classrooms with teachers who have difficulty maintaining classroom control.

These principals, however, will soon lose the respect of the outstanding teachers in their schools, who perceive him as weak and too afraid or incompetent at confronting and helping teachers who have difficulty maintaining classroom control. Teachers learn quickly that if they do their jobs exceedingly well the reward is more work and a tougher assignment.

Those teachers who complain about or refuse to become skilled at working with challenging students get rewarded by not having to work with these students. The end result of this deliberate administrative decision is an inequitable teacher workload.

The outstanding teachers then begin to question these principals' integrity, which will soon erode their ability to be seen as effective leaders. They also begin to resent those teachers whom they perceive receive unjustified preferential treatment from the boss. There will also be an increase in defiant or passive-aggressive behavior by the great teachers because they have observed that this strategy works.

Now the principals really have a conundrum. Initiating action against staff members can make them very unpopular with their colleagues and the community, especially if the staff members are well liked. It is however a key part of the job. Staff personnel need to be held accountable, and that is one of your primary responsibilities.

So what do you do with a staff member who does not do what you want him or her to do? First of all, the most critical element in the process is to identify the issue. In other words, what in specific terms is the conduct/attitude that you see as the issue?

The vital piece to the process of changing the behavior is to be able to describe the behavior to the person so clearly that she or he undoubtedly understands what your concern is. Although attitude is sometimes hard to define, you can identify those behaviors that result in your determination of the attitude you find unacceptable.

The overriding question is, *What in specific terms is the unacceptable conduct/attitude that you see as the issue, and how would you describe it to them that they understand what you mean?* There are some key questions that can assist you in identifying whether there is an issue.

1. *What harm is caused by their conduct/attitude?* Maybe it is just something that bothers you, but has no real impact on teaching and learning. For example, they do not attend any extracurricular activities to watch students perform. If that is the case, don't do anything. On the other hand, if they are failing a significantly high number of students from a particular demographic group, then that is an issue.

2. *Is it a recent issue or old and ongoing?* For example, if the individuals have had problems dealing with students with challenging behaviors for a while, then it needs to be addressed. If they recently have had some personal issues, such as the need to assist aging parents, that do not allow them to serve on committees, then it may not need to be addressed.
3. *Is this a private issue/situation, or does it have broader school/community implications?* If a team is not getting along and students are hearing one teacher criticize other members of the team in class, that is a problem that has to be addressed. If one counselor differs philosophically with the director of guidance and it does not impact students directly, then it probably can be dealt with in a less urgent manner.
4. *Is there some situation surrounding the activity of the individuals that might excuse them?* You are concerned that a new teacher is not utilizing the technology skills you know she possesses in her teaching. Your hopes were that she would help the seasoned members on the team who were reluctant users although you never told the team that. What you don't know is that the other team members feel threatened by her skills and openly put her down in front of students and other colleagues. There is a reason for her behavior—intimidation from colleagues. The issue that needs to be addressed here is not the teacher's behavior but rather the behavior of her colleagues.
5. *Is this a single incidence or indicative of a pattern?* Unless the issue is egregious or outrageous, we are not so much concerned with onetime incidents. Everybody says, texts, or does something he or she would like to take back. Mistakes are part of the learning process, so every action/behavior on the part of staff is not a life-or-death issue. However, if a staff member has a long list of complaints from students charging that he or she is demeaning to them in providing verbal feedback and nothing has been done, then that is an issue.
6. *If the issue has been identified previously, what help was provided to address the problem, what evidence is there of this, and was it successful?* If you are a new principal, the first place you look is in the individual's personnel file. If something happened, there should be documentation. This also may give you some clues as to whether it is an old and ongoing issue. In most instances, there is probably nothing in the file that will give you any helpful clues.

After you have clearly identified the issue/problem, the next step is to look at several key action questions before deciding to proceed.

1. *What if you did nothing to address the issue?* Will you ignore it because the teacher has only eight months to retirement and the prob-

lem will go away after she or he leaves? Or you may be hoping that the teacher wins the lottery and quits on Monday. The real question is, do you need to deal with it to resolve it or will it go away with no intervention on your behalf? Most of the time, willful neglect is not an effective change strategy.
2. *Is it worth the time and energy to address the issue?* The reality is staff issues consume a great deal of time and effort on your part and probably others' who will be assisting. Associated with this action may come the stress of having to deal with the dismissal process. In a confrontational process, it will at times feel like you are on trial, as you will have to defend your actions. Do you really want to do this?
3. *Will you have the support of the superintendent and school board?* If after doing your homework and determining this issue rises to the level where action is required, in the end will the superintendent and board defend your actions? Are there some politics in play that might make this staff member untouchable, for example, being a relative of a board member, town hero, or successful coach? It is better to know up front rather than to do all this work and then have the rug pulled out at the end. Without this support, your work goes nowhere. Even worse, the staff will know, and your ability to influence unacceptable staff behavior will have been compromised.
4. *Are there assessment and accountability systems in place?* Strong, well-run school systems will have three distinct assessment and accountability systems designed for staff. The first system is for those new to the district and is used to determine whether this individual should be granted a continuing contract or tenure after a set period of time. The second system is for those staff on continuing contracts or tenure for whom continued employment is not an issue. Their primary purpose is to promote professional growth in which the teacher is a full participant. The third model is for those staff who have a pattern of deficiencies or concerns that require intervention. This intervention can lead either to a change in staff behavior, which is the primary intent, or dismissal. If this model is present, then your difficult work has been made much easier. If this system is not in place, then proceed cautiously or not at all.
5. *What mentor/resource help will be available to you?* It is no secret that the primary reasons there are underperforming and incompetent staff in schools is that changing difficult staff behavior is complex and difficult work. The reality is many leaders lack the expertise to do the work that is necessary to manage all the steps competently and with integrity. You need the assistance of not only legal experts but also other individuals who have had experience as school leaders in doing this work. The areas where school leaders make mistakes are not

usually legal in nature. Most shortfalls are usually in clearly identifying issues, such as being an unwilling or uncooperative team member, developing meaningful action plans, and knowing how to communicate all of this to the staff member in a competent and respectful manner. Clarifying and carefully delineating performance issues requires a sophisticated degree of skill and knowledge.

6. *Do you have credibility as a leader?* Of all the questions to ponder before acting, this may be the most important. What reputation have you earned with staff, colleagues, and the community? Are you seen as a highly competent individual who has a reputation for always doing what is best for students and staff? Are you perceived as a strong leader who respects and is respected by staff? Are you regarded as someone who is thoughtful in your actions and fair in deliberations and treatment of staff and students? Do you have integrity?

    When you have to deal with a difficult staff member, many will be watching all your movements. If you have a solid reputation, those whose opinions count will know that you don't act in an arbitrary and capricious manner. They will believe that if you are taking action against an individual you must have a good reason, because they trust you.

    With mediocre and low-performing staff it, will not matter. Don't worry about them. Be concerned only about what your best teachers will think. In most instances, they are glad that you are taking action and probably wondering why it hasn't happened sooner. Weak staff help bring everyone down. Your job is to make everyone stronger. But you can do that only if you are perceived as a strong leader. And you can do that only by acting professionally, with integrity, and building that reputation on a teacher-by-teacher basis. Most staff will determine your competence based on how you treat them and consequently whether they can trust you. Trust is earned, not given.

After you have identified the issue and decided to act, you need to understand what the rationale is for the staff members' behavior before you can develop any action plan to remedy the situation. What is their motivation for acting this way? Here are five possible reasons:

1. They don't know what you want them to do.
2. They don't have the skills to do what you want them to do.
3. They don't see the importance of doing what you want them to do.
4. They don't want to do what you want them to do.
5. They have learned they don't have to do what you want them to do.

Let's look more closely at each one.

THEY DON'T KNOW WHAT YOU WANT THEM TO DO.

Many times, principals avoid confronting individuals or are not clear with expectations. You look in their personnel files, and there is no documentation regarding the matter. There is no mention on any evaluation materials that they have been told they need to take any action. If you have not communicated your concern, then you cannot hold them accountable. In this situation what do you do as principal? You clearly articulate to them what you want them to do and make sure they understand. If they don't know what you want them to do, it is unreasonable to expect them to do it.

THEY DON'T HAVE THE SKILLS TO DO WHAT YOU WANT THEM TO DO.

When you observe them in the classroom expecting to see integrated curriculum units with associated rubrics but they have had no training or experience with these things, how can you expect to see them? For them, it is safer to continue doing what they have been doing than to try something new. In this situation, what do you do as principal? You provide the prerequisite training opportunities and resources needed to get them the skills necessary to do the work you are expecting. They cannot do what they do not know how to do.

THEY DON'T SEE THE IMPORTANCE OF DOING WHAT YOU WANT THEM TO DO.

You have proposed that all teachers will have an advisory group this year as a way to better connect with students and serve as mentors. They argue that this is not the role of a teacher but rather the job of guidance counselors. They enthusiastically point out that if they wanted to have been guidance counselors they would have been. They teach science. In this situation, what do you do as principal? You provide them with information about their comprehensive role as teachers and closely monitor their work, offering support and encouragement. If they don't see why an action is important, you need to make it clear why it is.

THEY DON'T WANT TO DO WHAT YOU WANT THEM TO DO.

These issues become more difficult to deal with and elevate the task and stakes to a higher level. There can be many reasons for the defiance. It may be a philosophical difference or a willingness issue. For example, they may not believe that all staff need to have a web page to keep parents informed, or they may not want to do the extra work required to keep it current. In this situation, what do you do as principal? You need to tell them what they are expected to do and that it is not an optional assignment. This process may include performance outcomes, activities, resources and supports, assessment criteria, and a time line. It most likely will also include training opportunities. You need to be direct and supportive but make clearly known that not doing so is not an option. In the end, you may have to remind them that as an employee of the district, like yourself, they are not volunteers. Not doing what is requested is not a choice they have.

THEY HAVE LEARNED THAT THEY DON'T HAVE TO DO WHAT YOU WANT THEM TO DO.

If you have been the administrator in the building for a while, you are going to have a difficult, if not impossible, time getting them to change their behavior. They have learned that under your command they don't have to do something they don't want to and you will do nothing about it. You have earned a solid reputation for avoiding difficult staff issues, so why would they take you seriously now? In this situation, what do you do as principal? In reality, probably nothing you propose will be taken seriously. You have lost your credibility with them and probably with others. Your best option might be to seek other employment. If you are new, it is an easy solution. Why is it easy? Every time there is a new leader, the rules change. Past norms and ways of doing business and interacting with each other don't apply. With a new leader in the building, new expectations are determined and made known. You need to remind them that there are new rules and expectations.

Many times, we lament the behavior of staff without trying to figure out why they are acting or not acting a certain way. Or worse, we recognize what is wrong and choose not to act. In this scenario, no one wins, and in fact everyone loses. Most people who choose to work in schools—teachers, counselors, and social workers alike—want to work in a building that provides genuine assistance and resources for them to grow and flourish.

You must assume that all people strive to be the best they can be. They also deserve to work in a building where those needing assistance will respectfully receive it and those who are not performing up to standards are moved to positions where they can succeed or are, if necessary, dismissed.

Highly professional staff members understand that for the school to be a place where all students and staff are successful, only competent and caring staff members are allowed to come to work every day. No one else is allowed in the building. Savvy principals understand this and take action to ensure that this is the reality.

Chapter Nine

How May I Contact You? Let Me Reduce the Ways

Let's be totally frank. If you are a school principal, there are too many ways people can communicate with you. At times, it has to feel as though there is no escape from work; you're always on call. Unless the power goes out, your cell phone battery dies, or you're in a dead zone, there is no hiding. And often, with each interaction comes a request for you to respond in some manner.

Some requests are not complicated and take little time to address. For example, a community member wants to know where a particular meeting you are facilitating is being held. Or a member of the media wants to take a picture of the crew members of an upcoming play.

Others, however, may require lengthier, well-thought-out, detailed replies such as a parent asking why your school has discontinued the practice of tracking? Or perhaps a board member wants to know why all students are not allowed to take AP classes if they wish.

Many requests, because of the sensitive nature of the content, require you to respond, when, in fact, someone else could handle it just as well and, in many instances, better. To make matters more stressful, most people expect your response to be immediate, if not sooner.

We have become a society that expects instant answers to our questions. How many times do we search for the answer online, expecting instant results? As such, many parents or staff members do not understand why a reply is not forthcoming within minutes, sometimes seconds, after a request is sent. This is most apparent after we have texted someone.

Frequently, we stare at our phones expecting to hear a little noise and see an envelope at the top. We may even do this when we are driving despite the fact that this practice is outlawed in many states. We have developed the habit of being hooked to our smartphones.

To be able to get back to the sender so quickly implies that you are available. This assumes that you, in fact, have been waiting patiently for their e-mail, text, or call and anticipate quickly responding. Let's face it. Most e-mails/texts are not of the magnitude that would require you to stop everything you are doing to reply.

If you can respond that quickly to all the e-mails, my question is, what are you not doing that lets you respond that quickly? If you are in classrooms having a conversation with a teacher or meeting with a parent or civic group, then how are you available? If you are doing nothing, then you are available. If nothing else, not being immediately available may show you are doing something. And that is a good perception for people to have of you.

It is right to be a little suspicious of people who boast that they are always available. Some people confuse an open-door policy with always being available. An "open door" policy is a philosophy rather than a literal translation. It means you welcome ideas and look forward to working collaboratively with the best interests of the students and community at the center. It does not mean that your door is always open so people can come in whenever they want.

There are some principals who have open scheduling, which means their administrative assistants (AAs) or secretaries maintain their schedules, and if there is an opening, someone can take it. That is a different type of availability and may be appropriate in some situations to present the idea that you are accessible and want to interact with staff members. It does not mean you are always available.

Therefore, it could be strongly inferred that always being available when your boss contacts you is not a good thing. If you can always respond on the spot your boss will/should wonder what you are doing or if you indeed are doing anything. Even if you are available when people contact you at school, it is usually best for your secretary to say you are not. Have your secretary inform the people you are engaged in a meeting and ask whether they would like for her or him to find you. If they call on your smartphone or text, don't always answer or text right back.

Some clarification is needed here. I am not proposing that you lie to your boss. I am implying that you should be in the school and doing something. And it is OK to be available once in a while, just not all the time.

Aren't you supposed to be working? Superintendents like principals who are active in the school and visible in the community. Get back to them in a reasonable amount of time, and explain why you weren't available. It is a great way to inform them of how you are spending your time and to highlight your agenda. It also may prevent them from assuming that you can take on additional work because you have the time.

So how do you limit the access people have to you without appearing inaccessible, invisible, and/or disinterested in what people have to say or the issues they are facing? In developing strategies that will work, what you don't want to do is present the image that you are a leader who is not accessible or responsive to your constituents. That would be a public relations disaster and potentially career threatening. And you can never be rude, discourteous, or dishonest.

What you are attempting to do is manage how people connect with you so you can respond in a timely and thoughtful manner. You are not avoiding work but rather developing strategies to better maximize the use of your time. To help figure out how to manage all the ways people can communicate with you, let's examine how people currently contact you so we can reduce, modify, or eliminate some of those access points.

Let me count the ways they can access you now:

1. *In person.* They see you in the hall or a local store or at meetings, appointments, and games.
2. *E-mail.* They have access with no boundaries, twenty-four hours a day, seven days a week.
3. *Mail.* Not as great as in the past, but still an option.
4. *School phone.* They call and ask to speak to you.
5. *School voice mail.* They call, you are not there, and they leave a message, sometimes very long.
6. *Smartphone/text.* The school provides one for you, and people quickly learn the number, again providing access twenty-four hours a day, seven days a week.
7. *Smartphone voice mail.* They call to speak to you, you don't answer because you are celebrating your child's birthday, and they leave a long message.
8. *Home phone.* This should not be public, but if you live locally some will know it.
9. *Home phone answering machine.* They leave a message.
10. *Smartphone and school phone texting.* They leave a text.
11. *School web page blog.* They respond to your posts.
12. *Facebook.* The school district wants you to have one, and people want to be your friend.
13. *Twitter.* You have an account.
14. *Skype.* Works when parents are at a distance and not able to attend in person.

If you stop to think about it, just a few years ago this list was considerably shorter. With rapid technological advances, the list will continue to grow. So what can you do to be more in charge of this already out-of-control situation? The answer is simple. Limit, modify, or eliminate some of the access points.

After figuring out what will work in your situation, thoughtfully and sincerely communicate that information to all your constituents—students, parents, staff, and community. In doing so, it is critical that you explain how these changes actually provide greater, not less, access to you.

Most people will understand the rationale for such changes if it is clearly described to them. Many of them are probably experiencing the same problems in their personal or professional lives as you are. The ones that don't understand or agree probably have unrealistic expectations for your time and will criticize you no matter what you do. Don't worry about them. So how can you better manage the technological challenges? Here are a few suggestions:

DON'T HAVE A FACEBOOK, BLOG, OR TWITTER ACCOUNT, PERIOD.

They take up too much of your time and can only get you in trouble. For the most part, creating a blog and posting on it is an egocentric activity unless it has a definite purpose, like getting feedback on a book you are writing or commenting on issues of local concern. With respect to Facebook, very few really care who your favorite band is, what you are having for lunch, or what your uncle in North Dakota is doing for his sixtieth birthday.

If you have a strong desire to be on Twitter, you should have been a rock star. And how does that usually work out for them? Do you really think people are waiting patiently on hold to be inspired by what your next tweet will be all about? Many staff members lose their jobs each year over inappropriate photos, comments, or personal messages on social media.

If you have extra time, you should spend it with your family. If you choose to set up a blog, Facebook, or Twitter account, explain to your family and friends why this is so critical to your being successful as a principal. As you are doing that, explain to them why spending time with these activities is a better use of your time than spending time with them. If you have a personal Facebook account for family and friends, make sure it's password protected well and with high enough security that you can't be searched for online.

LET THE SECRETARIES SCREEN YOUR SCHOOL E-MAIL.

You heard right! Have it all forwarded to them and let them screen e-mail as they do your regular mail and phone calls. Where appropriate, they can forward it to you, reply themselves and cc you, or forward it to someone who can better respond. It would be safe to assume that when people find out your secretary is viewing all your e-mails, the number you receive will significantly be reduced. People will be forced to become more thoughtful and deliberate before hitting send if they know it is not going to you directly.

ELIMINATE SCHOOL VOICE MAIL.

Tell people you want to get back to them as soon as you can but it takes time to check all the ways people contact you on a daily basis. Limiting the number of ways is one strategy you can use to get back to them sooner. Also, it takes less time to leave a long message than it does to write one. Hence, you may also get fewer e-mails.

HOLD FIVE-MINUTE MEETINGS.

Thirty minutes before classes begin each day (maybe two or three times a week) be available for meetings that take less than five minutes. Sit on a bench in a highly visible part of the school and meet with whoever comes by. If nothing else, it will increase your visibility with students and staff. Principals who use this strategy report that the number of actual scheduled appointments has been reduced. In addition, staff members are commenting on how much faster they can get answers to simple questions. Everyone wins with this simple strategy.

LIMIT VISITING HOURS.

Set firm time parameters on when you do not respond to anyone. It could be from 5:00 p.m. on Friday to 7:00 a.m. on Monday. Also, set times during the week when you are no longer on the clock, even when you are home. Have your family help you with this. You need to have time that is not work time.

DON'T LIVE WHERE YOU WORK.

I know this is a controversial one (discussed in more detail in another chapter) for some people and hard to avoid if you live in some geographic areas. The simple, indisputable fact is that not living in the same community where you are employed will cut down dramatically on the number of personal contacts you have during evenings and weekends. It is also easier for your family, children, and friends. If you meet a student, parent, or board member at the grocery store who asks you a question, it is difficult to tell her or him you are not at work and to make an appointment. If you are not in the community during your nonworking hours, it is much easier to not have to deal with work 24/7.

The balance between people having access to you, which is critical to performing the responsibilities of your position, and having "a life" can be a fine one. With rapid technological advances in communication media, most of which are an asset to the principal, expectations for accessibility have changed. How the principal manages those expectations is a key to his or her success.

How many hours each day should you be expected to be accessible to your staff and the public, and when does your day end are key questions. How many hours a day can you work and be productive?

Time away from work is very important for you to rejuvenate and reenergize for the next day. This is a crucial issue that needs to be discussed by school boards and superintendents so principals can have realistic expectations for job performance.

In reality, discussions around these very important questions are not being held because neither boards nor superintendents want to have the answers made public. It is safe to assume that if these issues are not discussed, principals will either move to other districts or their professional and personal lives will suffer. In either situation, the outcome is not good and could have been prevented. It would behoove you when applying for a position to get a sense of what the district's expectations are in this area.

Savvy leaders learn to use communication strategies to lessen their workloads and enhance their performance. They are in control of how others communicate with them and how they interact with others. They also learn to use technology to help shape the perception external constituents have of them and the school.

Let's look at a horrendous example of a school leader sending the wrong message to those contacting the school and how changing that greeting can result in big dividends.

THE UNWELCOME GREETING

"Thank you for calling Impersonal Senior High School. Our office hours are 7:15 a.m. to 4:15 p.m., Monday through Thursday, and 7:00 a.m. to 4:00 p.m. on Fridays. If you know your party's extension, you may dial it at any time. Please press the pound sign to access the company directory. Please listen carefully to the following options:

- For the attendance office press 1.
- For the guidance office press 2.

- For the assistant principal's office press 3.
- For the athletic director's office press 4.
- For the principal's office press 5.
- For the school nurse press 6.
- For the IT office press 7.
- For the Vocational-Technical Center press 8.
- For the kitchen press 9.
- For the bus garage hang up and dial xxx xxxx.
- For the business office hang up and dial xxx xxxx.
- For the Special Services office hang up and dial xxx xxxx.
- For the superintendent's office hang up and dial xxx xxxx.
- If you know the first three letters of the last name of the person you are trying to contact, you may press those keys now.
- To reach an operator dial 0.
- To hear this message again press 10.
- Thank you for your call

If you know your party's extension, this taped message is not a problem for you, or is it?

What is the impression you want to send to parents and community members about your school when they call? Try this—it took one minute and fifteen seconds to get to the message that tells callers how they can speak with a real person in real time. If the point you are trying to convey is we are too busy to answer your call and we hope you get frustrated and hang up, or you want them to wonder if they called their credit card company, then you have succeeded.

In our attempt to use technology to help with efficiency and effectiveness, sometimes we use technology inappropriately. Having a canned, recorded response may be more efficient in terms of staff time required to answer the phone and respond, but it is not more effective in terms of public relations and customer service.

A recording is cold, impersonal, and frustrating. If that is the impression you want to send, then you have succeeded. Remember, most people are not calling the school just to chat. They are not calling a talk show. They are almost always calling to get or give information about their child. They are not calling for something to do, although some may appear at times to be doing just that.

What should you do? Very simply, have a live person answer the phone. Most of the time, people call schools to get information, leave a message, or seek help. If your staff members are not able to answer the phone, then involve your students, depending on their age. Phone etiquette skills are important to learn, especially in the age of texting.

Some schools I visit have student greeters in the front hallway. Their job is to welcome visitors in a friendly manner and channel them to the right staff member or office. They set a nice welcoming tone that students are an important part of this school.

If students are not a viable option, then there is a cadre of volunteers in the community to be tapped. Contact the chamber of commerce, Rotary, or other civic groups to help identify individuals who might be able to help. Connect with local senior citizen groups. Nursing facilities have activities directors whose job it is to find engaging things for their residents to do.

Having spent considerable time over the past few years visiting these establishments, I know there are many terrific seniors who would love this opportunity and would be great at it. There are many wonderful seniors who are still looking to be productive, contributing members of their community. They are not only a great resource, but their positive involvement in your school may help at budget times. You may even find a mentor or a "grandparent" for students or staff members who need one.

Your parent advisory committee could also assist with finding volunteers. Schools are always looking for positive opportunities to involve parents, and this is certainly one. The more people involved, the better.

Schooling is a personal relationship business in which considerate human interaction is important. Parents and visitors want to feel welcome and comfortable when they call the school. Have a friendly voice answer the phone. Set a good first impression that this school is a welcoming, friendly place where time is taken to be polite and considerate. Having a real person answer the phone sends the message you care as principal.

So get rid of the long, impersonal message. Try this instead: "Hello. Welcome to Friendly High School. This is Andrew. How may I help you?" That only takes four seconds, but the goodwill lasts much longer.

Chapter Ten

Only Hire Superstars

The most critical responsibility of the savvy principal is to find, recruit, and hire staff members who have a history of being exceptional. If that is not possible for each staff opening, the only other viable option is to find those individuals who have the potential to be superstars. There is absolutely nothing else you will do as principal that comes even remotely close to having such an impact (positive and negative) on students, parents, yourself, and ultimately test scores.

Great coaches do not win championships with average or unskilled players. They might make the tournament on occasion, but they will not consistently win. There is no doubt that great coaching helps make the talent better. But great coaching alone is not enough to produce championships. If you have to choose between the two, always choose talent. Fortunately, the savvy principal realizes that it is not an either/or situation.

Let me give you an example. Did you ever notice that coaches do not retire or resign if they have a championship team ready for the next season? They are not foolish. They always bail out when they know there is a significant talent drop. They go out on top. The poor coach that follows them, usually a new coach hunting for his or her first head coaching position, takes the hit. Community members who are not in the know will lament the loss of the esteemed coach at the expense of the rookie. The former coach understood the rules of success. Talent usually trumps coaching.

So why don't all principals understand this? Frankly, I don't know. If you think about all the problems principals have to deal with each day, they are not usually the result of the behavior of your outstanding staff members. Almost all of the students who are sent to your office do not come from the classrooms of your outstanding teachers.

Most of the calls you get from parents expressing concern about a teacher's actions are not concerns about the behaviors of outstanding teachers. Most of the problems that students may have with each other that result in their being sent to your office are not found in classrooms of outstanding teachers. And, finally, most of the issues that teachers have with each other are not issues between outstanding teachers.

So how do you go about finding, recruiting, and hiring great staff? The first and most obvious strategy is to have a school where everyone wants to work. If you create a culture and reputation that your school is a terrific place for adults and students to learn and work, exceptional staff will find you. If you have developed a school culture where staff members are treated with respect at all times, that will be evident, particularly within your system/district. Many of the outstanding staff members that I hired over the years came from other buildings in the district. I most truthfully admit, it did not always make me popular with other principals.

If your school has been recognized for outstanding achievement or innovation or is known for a particular focus (e.g., expeditionary learning), that will help get the word out. The more good press you receive, the better. It is also a plus for staff members to attend and present at conferences—state, regional, and national. Only in the past couple of decades has it been acceptable for public schools to aggressively market themselves. Competition from private, charter, and for-profit schools has made that possible and practical.

Great places to work don't happen by chance. They are primarily the result of the deliberate and thoughtful actions on the part of the leader. It helps if the values and success of the school are clear and well known. If you establish a positive reputation that is well earned, word will get out. But even that is not enough.

Every time you have an opening in your school, you must carefully examine what qualifications you are seeking in the candidate. You are not simply hiring a body to replace another body. What skills, knowledge, expertise, experiences, and potential are you looking for? How is this person going to add to your stable of superstars? How will you ensure you have found the best possible candidate? Here are some ideas to consider.

Clearly define the opening that exists. Do not shortcut this process. If you lose a ninth-grade science teacher, are you going to replace that person with another ninth-grade science teacher or create another position of greater need? Too many times, principals don't think about the opportunity an opening creates, and they take the safe route.

Maybe you don't need another science teacher, but rather the school has a greater need for a student advocate or a high school completion coordinator. If the school administration has a clear plan and focus, when an opening occurs, they know which staffing is needed next. And it could be the primary need is a ninth-grade science teacher.

Although the principal ultimately makes the final call, the more staff members you involve in the process, the better. It helps to create the feeling that your school is a special place in which people want to work. It reinforces the belief that staff input is valued and encouraged within structured protocols.

The process is neither haphazard nor random. The staff members are helping to determine who is going to be joining them. It reinforces the message that it is a privilege to work in this school and those who work here take pride in determining who their new colleague will be. Lean on your outstanding staff to be highly involved in this process.

An opening is a rare opportunity and should be treated as such. It is a chance to improve the talent pool. The goal should be to hire someone who is better than, or has the potential to be better than, 90 percent of your current staff. I will not attempt to define "better than" here, but it can be assumed that these are the staff members that make you look really good as leader. These are the top-notch teachers.

After you have clearly identified the staff need, think further about what will be included on the job description. This is your advertisement. It should not be vague and uninteresting. What type of high flyer wants a vague and dull-looking job? It needs to be thoughtful, engaging, and descriptive beyond the usual stuff found in typical boring ads that typical boring, run-of-the-mill schools create. You need to create some excitement in your ad.

What makes your school different, and why would someone of high competence be interested in looking at what you have to offer? You have to make your school appealing to attract the widest possible talent pool from which to choose.

The next consideration is how you are going to get the word out that you have an opening. How are you going to get the greatest exposure? There are the traditional routes, which are the colleges that have job placement services. If you have contacts at any of these institutions, call on them; a personal contact is always helpful. These contacts can save you a great deal of time, especially in identifying new talent.

The only caution here is that you do not want to hire too many individuals who graduated from the same institution. Why is that? Simply speaking, the greater diversity in background and experience there is in staff members' education, the greater diversity of thinking there should be in your school.

Most colleges/universities and departments within colleges/universities have a particular philosophy or focus in their education and training. For example, there are science departments in brand colleges that give grades in chemistry classes based on a curve. All students could have grades above 90, yet some would get A's, while others only a point lower would get C's.

There are other institutions of higher learning where students design their individual programs of study and most classes are offered pass/fail. There are also colleges that focus on interdisciplinary, collaborative learning and producing graduates that think creatively. This rich blend of experiences helps to create a melting pot of perspectives that can only serve to add to the individual professional growth of staff and the resulting diverse experiences students receive.

Technology can play a key role in getting your vacancy out to the widest audience possible. Many school systems contract with specific job websites. The advantages are that they are usually low cost and offer high visibility. Most can be updated easily, and the electronic filing of applications is quick and cost effective.

If you know other principals who may be in a reduction in force situation, you may get a lead on some terrific novice talent beginning their careers. Or they may have an outstanding experienced staff member that is looking for new opportunities to jump-start his or her career, and you may have that perfect situation.

It is uncommon for superintendents to reach out to other superintendents when looking for principals, but it is rarer for principals to ask each other about potential teachers. If you are a member of a principal professional association, asking your colleagues is a good place to start.

Use your outstanding teachers as recruiters. Maybe they have friends in other buildings or districts that are looking to leave where they are. My experience has been that people who think and act alike tend to hang out together. Just as gossipers and whiners tend to spend time together, so do great teachers. Maybe your top staff members know individuals from their involvement in professional associations (art educators) or volunteering (Boys and Girls Clubs of America).

What is the next step after you have a pool of candidates? There should be some sort of rubric that allows you to identify those candidates you want to interview. The rubric should be such that the best candidates are not eliminated because your rubric was faulty. It must meet rigid compliance standards established by your district human resource office, yet at the same time produce the best candidates. You can do this by weighting some categories more than others. Always leave yourself some room to maneuver.

This is similar to a question you would ask teachers about the assessments they use. For example, you would ask, do your best mathematicians get the best math grades? If not, why not? The same holds true for screening. Does your assessment system allow you to identify and interview the best candidates? If not, why not, and how do you know that it doesn't?

After you have identified the pool of potential employees, what is the structure of the selection process for making sure you get the right person to join the team and then getting him or her to commit to accepting the position? If you are an outstanding organization, you must do things a little differently from every other school. The process must be innovative and get the desired outcome.

A goal should be to get feedback from as many different people as possible. You could find ways to involve staff at various points as long as there is a core of staff, yourself included, that sees the candidates at all the key points. For example, someone could meet the candidates as they arrive at the school and serve as their host; another could take them on a tour, while others could do the interviewing.

A good first step is to Skype candidate interviews. Give candidates fifteen to thirty minutes to respond to set questions that you sent them before the interview. This would provide an opportunity to see candidates and measure how they do when given time to think about an issue ahead of time. You could also leave time to ask them follow-up questions to clarify or add to any comments they made. It also allows different groups of staff to view different candidates.

If candidates are from a distance, it also allows them to give you a first impression without having to travel to your district. It shows concern for their time and money. You can also eliminate candidates who may look good on paper but whose presence does not correlate well with their submitted materials. In the end, it saves the candidate and school additional time if you do not view them as serious candidates. They likewise may choose to withdraw.

If you have a number of potentially outstanding candidates, I would suggest group interviews. This is a strategy whereby two to three staff members interview three or four candidates together at the same time. Instead of having one candidate at a time respond to questions, there are three or four responding. You would ask candidates the same questions and sometimes ask them to comment on what another candidate has said. You get them involved in a discussion. You must, however, like a moderator during a presidential debate, be sure that each candidate has an equal amount of time to present him- or herself to the interview committee.

I first conducted group interviews out of necessity, but it turned out to be one of the smartest decisions I ever made. At the time, I was the director of elementary education (principal) in a working-class community, and it was my first year. I was responsible for six K–3 schools, each with a population of around 250 students. There were approximately twenty classroom positions that needed to be filled for the upcoming year. The only thing I knew how to do at that time was one-on-one interviews.

There were hundreds of applications. The process I set up was to review the candidates myself, check my choices with the six teaching principals, make final selections on those to be interviewed, and then involve the teaching principals in the interview process. The teaching principals had full-day schedules and were eager to have me do the initial screening. I gave an initial list of twenty-five names to my secretary and asked her to set up interviews.

The next day, when I arrived at work, my list of twenty-five had expanded to about sixty. I was perplexed, so I asked her why. She told me that it was district policy that anyone who graduated from the local high school or who lived in town was granted an interview. Some she noted had been interviewed multiple times. I was in shock.

How could I be part of sixty interviews? How would I ever find the time? This was ridiculous. I went to the superintendent and asked him about the policy. He said it was true. I would have to interview every applicant with local ties. I asked whether there was any way around this. He said no.

I spent some time thinking about how I was going to do this and began to think of options. I could have different groups interview different candidates. That way I would not need to be in on every interview. But I wanted to be part of every interview because I realized the importance of these hires. So, although it would save time, it did not work for what I was trying to accomplish.

Then I thought of group interviews. Why not have four candidates interview at the same time? They could be asked questions, interact with each other, and be afforded the opportunity to comment on others' responses, all in a one-hour time block.

There were several advantages to this approach. One obvious advantage was that it would save me a ton of time. If one candidate was clearly not a fit, I did not waste an hour. Also, as I was hiring more than one person, it was possible that all four participants in a session could be hired. That relieved some anxiety on the part of the candidates.

Since all the positions required working in a small school in a team situation, I could analyze how they responded to others' comments. For example, were they respectful of others even if their position on an issue was the opposite? Did they appear to be listening to what others said? Did they look interested, or were they trying to make themselves look better by critiquing another's response?

I decided to ask the superintendent and assistant superintendent to sit in on all the interviews with me. I think they said yes because they did not have a good way of saying no. I also think that the fact that I was new and had no assistant was a factor.

I developed a scoring rubric that we used for all the candidates. After we scored them individually, we talked about who we would bring back for final interviews at the individual schools for the teaching principals to interview. When the applicant went to the school level, I worked with the teaching principals to select and recommend the finalists to the superintendent.

Even though I stumbled on to the process, it worked great, and I have used it at other times when appropriate. The candidates all were told ahead of time about the process. I can recall only a couple of candidates withdrawing their applications as a result. That decision probably saved us both time and energy.

There was also another side benefit of the process. That was the last year the policy of granting interviews to anyone in town that applied for a position was enforced. The superintendent decided to change it. I later learned that it was not an official board policy but rather a historical practice.

Another strategy for finding the best candidates is to make the process as realistic as possible. If possible, ask the candidates to do what they will be doing. If they are going to teach history in an interdisciplinary setting, ask them to teach a lesson to an appropriate group of students.

At one time in my career, I was the director of alternative education for grades 6–12. This basically meant that I directed and oversaw any programs that were not considered part of the traditional school offerings. Some programs were on campus, housed within school buildings, while others were in offsite facilities. In either situation, home visits were a requirement and frequent travel to all parts of town a necessity.

And some of these places you had to visit were in areas where it could be deemed not safe. One particular venue that some of my high school students liked to hang out at was a pool hall/game facility. I was comfortable going there, but some of the former alternative education teachers were not. I knew the manager well, and he knew I was trying hard to keep the kids who hung out there in school. He would work with me because he knew I cared and that for some of these students it was their last chance to complete high school.

As part of the interview process, I would take final candidates around town to show them where some of the students lived and hung out. I would always stop at this establishment to visit with my friend, the owner, and to play a game of pool. I would closely observe how comfortable they were being there. If they were not at ease being there with me, they were not likely to be going there alone to talk to the kids.

The manager knew exactly what I was doing and would often offer his opinion about a candidate after the interview. Many a candidate was eliminated after the visit. The trick is to find your pool hall that matches the position.

If the candidates are going to be teaching, it is always a good idea to have them teach a class. We would usually have them teach an existing class of students rather than assemble a group of students. It is also a really good way to get age-appropriate feedback from students. What did they like about the lesson? How did the candidate relate to the students?

In the end, there is no substitute for long conversations about philosophies of teaching and learning, examining beliefs about who can and cannot learn, thinking about what future students should be able to know and do, and getting to know candidates' aspirations. You cannot shortcut the process. It must be thoughtful and diligent. You must seek out and hire the best people you can find to add to the team.

Remember, you are better off with an empty classroom than one filled with a teacher who is not outstanding. The performance levels of below-average teachers only cause problems for students, parents, other staff, and yourself. And you don't have time for that.

It should go without saying that checking references is critical. No matter how carefully crafted and carried out the screening process is, you can get fooled. You need to check references listed and beyond if possible. I will give you a prime and sobering example of why this is so important.

I was working with one particular school system helping principals deal with staff issues. I would assist principals in learning how to observe and collect data to either help staff members improve or, ultimately, to assist them in pursuing the teachers' dismissal. I would also assist them with developing appropriate action plans.

There was one particular teacher who was a recent hire in an area of high need—science. Although there were some concerns, he had a strong and impressive résumé in the private sector, which most parents love. He was a graduate of a brand college and recent one-year teacher certification program, which had a strong reputation for producing graduates that were in demand.

In one of our meetings, the principal had expressed some concerns to me that this new teacher was not always open to suggestions. He projected an attitude that he knew his academic area and should be given more freedom to select what and how he was going to teach.

There were also some rumblings from students in his classes that he was not the most patient person and could be sarcastic at times. The principal was paying close attention to him and had to respond on more than one occasion to parents' complaints that he would make unflattering comments about their child in front of both of them and online.

One day near the end of the school year, another teacher came to the principal to ask her whether she knew what this teacher was using for a pass when students wanted to use the bathroom. The principal responded that she did not. The teacher said that this science teacher was having high school students carry a toilet seat from the classroom to the bathroom.

When confronted, the new teacher did not deny it. In fact, he saw nothing wrong with this requirement. He believed the students did not need to use the restrooms; they only wanted to get out of class. I wonder why that was? The principal tried to explain that this was humiliating for students and it was to cease immediately. The teacher reluctantly complied. Shortly, thereafter, the teacher resigned but completed the last two weeks of school. He knew he was not going to receive a contract for a second year.

The following September, I was in a high school twenty miles from this school. As I was walking around the building, I recognized a name on a door. It was the same name as the "toilet seat" teacher. I asked the principal who this person was. He said they were lucky to find him, as one week before school started one of the chemistry teachers resigned. I said nothing.

When I left the building, I called the principal who had previously had to deal with the toilet seat teacher. She had left her old position and remarkably had moved to another position as principal in the same district that had hired her old toilet seat chemistry teacher. I asked her if they had called her for a reference check. They had not.

Two years after being hired, this same teacher was fired during the school year for inappropriate conduct. That did not surprise me or his old principal.

There is no excuse for a principal not doing his or her homework, especially when the stakes are as important as hiring. If you cannot find an outstanding candidate, an empty classroom is sometimes the best alternative.

Your primary legacy as a leader is the staff members you leave behind at the school when you leave. It all starts with developing a process that ensures the best are hired. There is no other responsibility you have that is more important or critical to the success of the school and you.

Chapter Eleven

Enhance Your Reputation—Make Every Meeting Matter

If a laptop is open at a meeting at your school, does that mean the individual is

1. Carefully taking minutes of the actions and decisions being made?
2. Researching a question that has been raised?
3. Checking e-mails?
4. Ordering a sweater from an online retailer?

Chances are that, if your school is like most schools, the answer you selected is probably a choice between 3 and 4, when it should be 1 or 2. An all too frequent complaint from most school staff members is that they attend too many useless and unproductive meetings. These are gatherings where a lot is said but little is accomplished.

It is an occasion where people talk, don't say much, and then end up disagreeing after the meeting about what actually took place. And if the meetings are perceived as unproductive, then one must conclude that little meaningful work is accomplished in this setting. They are in fact poorly organized social events where too much valuable staff time is wasted.

An even more disturbing realization is that most of the work supposedly conducted in schools today is done collaboratively, which requires meetings. Hence, one is left to conclude that not much happens in these facilities. No standout leader in this building!

Unfortunately, principals facilitate many of these wasteful meetings. And how can that be? Do principals really not know what to do? Wouldn't you think that their experiences as teachers sitting in dreadful meetings would have taught them what to do when they are in charge? Did they forget? They must have had some instruction in graduate school in terms of effectively managing staff. There is even an ISLLC Standard 3, which talks about utilizing human resources wisely. Maybe their university professors had never actually been in charge of a school and had no practical experience to share. You can't teach what you don't know, and from my experience, university faculty meetings are not meeting models to be emulated.

How about consultants? There is no shortage of consultants eager to help for a fee. There are also hundreds of workshops each year on how to run effective meetings. If none of these options works for you time wise or financially, you can always read about it. A recent web search yielded nearly 1,500 books about how to run a meeting. Surely one of these publications has some information that will help you.

Given all that, what do you do? If you cannot run an effective meeting, you are toast. The same goes for not being able to run an assembly or organize a duty schedule. If you don't have a vision and cannot manage the day-to-day tasks of running a building, staff will never follow your leadership. If you can't manage the daily details that keep the school running smoothly, it tells everyone that you don't know how to implement the big picture. To achieve the big picture requires you to know and fill in the details required as part of the process.

There are basically three general types of meetings that take place in schools. The first and most important type is problem-solving meetings. In these gatherings, staff members are assembled and charged with solving problems, setting direction for the future, and making decisions. Examples would be school councils or department and team meetings. The important work of the school takes place in these meetings, and the focus is collaborative with all parties expected to actively participate.

A second type of meeting is for sharing or disseminating information. There may be details/information that is best conveyed face-to-face rather than online. An example of this would be a faculty group sharing the research work they had gathered on ways to place students in world language classes or the progress the math department is making on a standards-based model of instruction. The principal may have been required by the superintendent to update the staff on the status of the new building project, or there may have been a tragic incident involving a student. Again, the information needs to get out quickly, and staff members need be told at the same time so there is no chance of misinterpretation.

The third type of meeting is social/symbolic. It may be a staff recognition ceremony or an end-of-the-year celebration to honor retirees.

The sharing/disseminating information and social/symbolic meetings do not require the same level of skill as the problem-solving meetings; hence, we will focus on how to run great problem-solving meetings. If you do that well, the other two types are easy.

How you run a meeting tells everything about you as a leader. It illustrates to people how organized and focused you are. It provides key insights into what you believe about how you value their time and yours. Think about this for a moment.

For the sake of argument, let's fix the national average teacher salary in 2013 at $56,000. If we assume most teaching contracts are for 175 days and a day is defined as seven hours, then teachers earn $310.00 a day, or $46.00 an hour. I know most teachers work more than seven hours a day, but for my purpose, seven works. If you have fifty staff members gathered for a one-hour meeting, that meeting costs you $2,300.00 in staff time. You can adjust up or down depending on the size of your staff and whom you include. And that does not factor in your big salary or your assistants'. The point is it costs money to hold a meeting. If that money were coming out of your pocket, would you hold the meeting if it were not a productive one?

Let's look at it from a different perspective. Assume you are building a house. You have decided to hold a meeting with all those who are going to be involved in the project, and you have to pay them their hourly rate to attend. At this meeting will be an architect, head contractor, two plumbers, two electricians, three carpenters, one painter, a mason and his helper, the landscaping contractor, and the driveway installer. You need to make sure they are all on the same page and that the work and schedules will be coordinated and integrated seamlessly.

You need to be certain they are building the same house, not a series of rooms/parts that you hope come together. Each subcontractor needs to know how the other peoples' work fits with what he or she is doing. Time is money, and you cannot afford change orders. Would you begin this meeting with no focus or expected outcomes? Would you not have strategies in place to make the best use of their time and yours?

Would you not want a process that allowed for each participant to contribute in a manner that would get you the best house, for the best price, in the most efficient and effective manner? Of course you would. You want this for two reasons: (1) you want a great house, and (2) you want to get the most for your money. You need to take that same attitude to work each day as the leader. Treat all utilization of resources, both human and monetary, as if you are spending your money.

OK, here's how you do it. Commencing at the first staff meeting, set the tone that you value their time as much as yours. As such you will be respectful of how meeting time is scheduled and utilized. At the first staff meeting, ask them two questions. First, what makes a great meeting? In other words, when you attend a meeting that is productive, what are the indicators that make it worthwhile. Have them write their responses individually and then share them together in small groups. Decide ahead of time how you want the groups to look. If you have no plan on how you want to put the groups together, then do it randomly. The responses you will get to the question will be something like this:

- We accomplished something.
- I felt listened to.
- People were on task.
- No one person dominated the conversation.
- There was food.
- We followed an agenda.
- It was not too long.
- People were on time.
- Decisions were made.
- There were no interruptions.
- No one was correcting papers or working on her iPad.
- I enjoyed working with the people.
- It was worth my time.

Make a list, or have someone help you, of every comment and ask if there are some common elements. It is very difficult to facilitate and take notes at the same time, as it slows down the process. Ask them what those common answers are. There will be many. This should take only a few minutes.

Second, ask them what percentage of meetings they attend that are great. From past experience, I would be surprised if the average response gets close to 50 percent. As a new leader, the lower the number, the more you will benefit. Why is that? If their experience with meetings has been horrendous, they will welcome someone who indicates up front that things will be better.

This goes along with the mantra of never following a standout leader. Why do you think that no one wants to follow a highly successful coach or teacher? You will always be compared to that person. It is far better to be compared to someone who was incompetent than someone considered a superstar.

Then ask staff whether these great meetings happen by chance. The universal answer is no. This is your opportunity to show them you care about them and that you are a leader who is organized. Seize the moment. Share with them that you are on the same page. You understand that great meetings don't happen by chance and that there are certain actions that need to be taken. Next ask them to consider the following:

For a meeting to be great, what specific things do the facilitator and participants need to do before, during, and after the meeting? Ask them to write three things that the facilitator and participants have to do at each phase. It is important to have participants write things down because it ensures that everyone participates. Remind them not to begin processing the information as a group until everyone has written at least three things.

Being that you are a new principal, everyone should be on his or her best behavior for a short time. If someone chooses not to participate in this writing activity, it gives you immediate insights about who may be problems as staff members. That is always valuable information to gain.

After each member in the small groups has written down three things, have the group decide by consensus what those behaviors are. It is important to provide a definition of consensus. Here is one I have used successfully: *I may not necessarily agree with the decision/action, but I can support it because it is logical and feasible.* This definition works for many reasons. People generally know that 100 percent agreement is not possible on every issue for many reasons that do not always make sense. If you put in the logical and feasible part, you get much further. For example, although you might like to use your iPad during meetings, you could understand that some may interpret this to mean that you may not be paying attention.

Once they have compiled the data in small groups for each of the six aspects, process this with the entire staff. Again go through each category using the same definition for consensus. You never vote. Let me say that again. You never vote. Why is that? My experience tells me that voting does not lead to building consensus for doing the work of the school or creating a sense of community. Voting leads only to staff divisiveness and a majority rules mentality. If you are going to vote on an issue, you don't need a leader.

Streetwise and savvy leaders do not hold votes. If you are thinking about voting, make the decision yourself. There are only two exceptions to the no voting mantra. Some grants require a certain percentage of the faculty to vote in favor of participating before money is awarded. You have no choice there. The second exception is what the food choices will be for lunch at a professional development day. If you vote in other situations, you abdicate your responsibility as a leader.

It is imperative that you facilitate this great meeting protocol activity for several important reasons. First of all, it models for staff that you are adept at running a meeting and getting consensus. It also lets you ask key questions throughout that others may feel uncomfortable asking. Being new, you can raise difficult questions because you have no history. That is also why you need to make this your first activity after taking a new position.

What can you expect for responses from staff about the responsibilities of the facilitator and participants? I did this exercise as a school leader and many more times while working with schools. Here is a list of the most common responses:

- Start and end on time
- Have an agenda ahead of time
- Review the agenda ahead of time
- Conduct one piece of business at a time

- Assign time limits to each agenda item
- Stick to the agenda as written
- Support, challenge, and confront ideas, not people
- Conduct group business in front of the group
- Show respect for others in the group by not doing e-mail, texting, searching the web, correcting papers, taking phone calls, doing crafts, or selling items for your child's fund-raiser
- Share the air—give all a chance to participate
- Avoid interruptions to the meeting
- Have food
- Utilize the different expertise in the group
- Recognize that participation is a right and a responsibility
- Make decisions
- Summarize what was decided
- Assign follow-up actions and responsibilities
- Set the next agenda
- Conduct meetings in private and comfortable spaces
- Have a process to assess and evaluate the effectiveness of decisions made
- Take time to value and recognize the contributions of members
- Agree on strategies to assess how effective the group is working together
- Do the most important items first

At the end of tabulating these responses ask, "Is there anything on this list that is not logical and feasible?" Most people will have no objections and in fact be relieved that there will be some protocols, with the hope that meetings will be more productive than in the past. You may also have a few people disagreeing with some items on the list (e.g., using laptops, but being unable to argue that using them is logical). If they verbally object, they may be viewed as being self-centered or obstructive. Most people do not want to look that way at the first meeting with the new leader, even if they are.

What you will end up with is not only guidelines on how to run effective meetings but norms about how adults will interact with each other. This is the primary intent of the exercise and the real victory for you and the staff. You will have demonstrated to the staff how staff will treat each other with a new leader in town. Remember, whenever there is a new leader all the rules change.

Another way to demonstrate in a respectful manner that you are an action person is to talk about how items will get placed/organized on an agenda. Each topic will be classified as a decision, a discussion, or an information item. Emphasize that the items to be dealt with first are those that require a decision at that meeting. You will do this because they are indeed the most important.

Next in order to be addressed would be discussion items, followed finally by information/announcements. Too many times meetings get bogged down with announcements, which turn out to be advocacy or discussion items, and no time is left to do the important work. You should state that, when feasible, announcement/information items will be sent electronically.

By doing decision items first, I can assure you that attendance at the beginning of meetings will improve. This is especially true if agenda topics are important and impact the work and lives of the staff.

A final note: always start and end on time. If you need to add time to the meeting, do it rarely and only with the approval of the group members. If someone has to leave, don't object. If you respect the fact that people have other responsibilities outside work, they will usually contribute more when at work. You will also get improved attendance if you follow this guideline of valuing your time and theirs.

This entire process need not take more than ninety minutes if organized and facilitated properly. The end result of this process will be your solidified image as a focused and considerate leader, guidelines for running all meetings at the building, and protocols for how staff will work together in a respectful and productive manner. From a cost perspective, you are demonstrating that the district got its money's worth when they hired you to be the savvy principal.

Chapter Twelve

What Your Office Tells Others About You

When a parent, student, or community member walks into your office, what does the physical appearance of your work space tell them about you? The design and decor of your office, intended or otherwise, will offer the visitor valuable insights into your values and beliefs. Whether or not you designed your space with a purpose, there are distinct impressions being made. Never thought about that before? Well, you should have! Want to figure out what impression people are getting?

Here is what you do. Go outside your building and follow the same route as someone who is coming to a meeting with you at your office. As you walk the route, ask yourself these five questions:

1. When you first walk in, what do you notice? Is there anything in particular that stands out to you—items, colors, layout?
2. What do you think the principal values?
3. What tone do you think the principal is trying to set?
4. What do you think the layout and setup of the office may say about the principal's attitude toward power and status and his or her preferred leadership style?
5. What is your overall impression of the space?

In the past twenty years, I have been in the schools and, more specifically, the offices of over one thousand principals, assistant principals, superintendents, assistant superintendents, directors of special education, and curriculum directors. During these many visits, I became keenly interested in the physical appearance of schools and offices and what messages, intended or otherwise, the design of the space tells the visitor about the values and beliefs of the administrators.

Actually my interest in the topic of how space design impacts learning and working goes back over thirty years. In a previous position, one of my responsibilities was overseeing the alternative education programs in a large district. With that came grant monies to build and design classroom spaces.

We hired an environmental psychologist from one of America's oldest institutions of higher education to assist us in designing classroom spaces for students who had not previously been successful in schools. We examined colors, shapes, and structures. I learned why stores have arches in certain departments. Arches supposedly are welcoming and draw people in. I learned that certain colors have the potential to set particular moods.

So what colors do you choose when you are trying to set a mood or tone in your office? Here is what I have gathered from all I have read and seen and from what my wife, Vanessa, who is an artist, told me.

Black implies power and authority and also can imply submission. Villains in movies and books wear black. My friend Roger Shaw, superintendent of schools and former basketball official, told me that the International Association of Approved Basketball Officials replaced the black/white referee shirt with a gray/white one because the black/white denoted stress, anger, and frustration. The gray was a neutral, soothing color. And referees would never want to be perceived as villains or wanting to do anything that would incite fans.

I must admit I have never seen an office with black walls, although I have seen many leaders drive black vehicles. If you don't want to be perceived as a villain, you might skip black as a color unless you intend to add black lights. If you choose to paint your office black, it might be logical to assume that it will be repainted within months anyway by your successor.

White is usually thought of as representing purity and innocence. It goes with everything but is hard to clean. Maybe that is why most principals' offices are white. The leader of the school stands for all that is good and pure about schooling. Or maybe it's because it's cheap to buy and easy to match.

Red is considered an intense color, causing emotions to rise. It is not good to wear if you are negotiating or trying to resolve a conflict. It is probably the last choice for adorning your walls. I have never seen a counselor's office with red walls or furniture or a customer service area in a business painted red. There must be a reason for that. My advice is to avoid red unless it is the school color, in which case, you could have a pennant on the wall instead.

Pink is thought to be a soothing color and also is seen as the color of romance. Again, it's probably not a good color for your office, especially the romance part. Wearing pink seems to be OK.

Blue is an interesting color. Depending on the hue and intensity, blue can be peaceful and calm or cold and depressing. It is sometimes suggested that people are more productive in blue rooms. Peaceful and calm sounds much better than cold and depressing. We have too much cold and depressing as it is and don't need any more, especially in the principal's office.

Green has become synonymous with nature. It is thought to be restful on the eye and can improve vision. If you ever wondered why most center field walls in baseball are painted green, now you know. It may not be a good thing for the pitcher, but it does help the batter pick up the spin on the ball. It is a calming, refreshing color and is thought to reduce stress. Hospitals often use green because it relaxes patients. Dark green is masculine and conservative and implies wealth.

Purple is thought to be the color of royalty, wealth, sophistication, and creativity. My next office will have purple walls.

Yellow is considered to be an optimistic color. Research indicates that it speeds up the metabolism and enhances concentration (which is why legal pads are yellow). When combined with black, the duo demands attention. Think school buses. Many are yellow and black because those colors get your attention quicker than any other combination of colors.

Brown is often considered to represent the ideas of solidity, earthiness, stability, durability, and sadness. This color would work if not for the tone of sadness. Coffins are usually brown in tone.

Orange denotes excitement, energy, and enthusiasm. It can radiate both vitality and warmth. Might be a good color for your office! Also said to stimulate the appetite, so it would make an excellent choice for the school cafeteria, especially if the food is so-so.

From my work with an environmental psychologist, I learned that the color of a room can also affect people's perception of temperature. Supposedly, tests document that people estimate the temperature of a room with cool colors, such as blues and greens, to be six to ten degrees Fahrenheit cooler than the actual temperature. Warm colors, such as reds and oranges, will result in a six- to ten-degree Fahrenheit warmer estimate. I think I would choose blues and greens. Maybe you could make the selection based on the region of the country in which you reside.

Let's now look at all the stuff you have placed in your office and how it is arranged. I have attempted to interpret what I have seen in over one thousand offices and analyze the message I think it sends about the leader. As with everything else in the book, there is no research or scientific basis to support my analysis. There are only my perceptions about how you may be perceived based on how your office looks.

Queen/King/Princess/Prince. Diplomas on wall in big frames, name plaque (mahogany with gold lettering) on desk with *Dr.* before your name, pictures with dignitaries on the walls, big chair and desk with you on one side and the visitors on the other, trophies and awards. New and classic hardcover (no paperback) books about leadership are behind you in mahogany bookcases. If you wrote a book or article, it is there for all to see. You may have a copy on your desk or table or framed on the wall in a prominent place. The space is very clean, with no clutter. Message: you are important; don't stay too long, as you have more important people to meet with.

Adventurer/Traveler. Pictures on walls about you on vacation at exciting places in the world—white-water rafting, sailing in the Caribbean, on a safari, at the Tower of London. Artifacts from around the world—masks from Africa, steins from England, prints from Japan. Office is about you when not at work. No school-related items such as yearbooks or school mascot. Message: you work here only to get funds to take your next adventure and that given a choice, you'd rather be someplace else.

Office Sitter/Short Termer. Like a house sitter, you don't plan to be here long. Office is filled with unpacked boxes piled in corners. Pictures are randomly placed on walls with no theme. There are carpet stains and files in unpacked boxes; chart paper is loosely hung on whiteboards. Chairs have books on them. Your coat is thrown over the bookcase. Looks like a garage sale. Mission statement hung on the wall is fading. No plants, family pictures. Message: You are either moving in or moving out. You are not invested in the school. It is a stepping-stone position or a placeholder until something better comes along.

Resident. Your office is neat and well organized. There are plants and pictures of your family carefully arranged on desks or walls. The room is welcoming, and comfortable chairs are situated such that you sit next to people, not across from them. There are no pictures of things. There may be a picture of groups of students working in the community. There are some school-related items proudly, yet tastefully, displayed. You have current books on school leadership, but they are paperback. Message: You are connected to the school and understand the culture of the community. You enjoy working and learning with others.

So given all this information, make a conscious and thoughtful decision about what you want the appearance of your office to say about who you are and what you value. What you don't want to happen is to have your office create unintended barriers to your doing your job.

The role of principal is difficult enough. You don't need people to see red before they see red. You want them to feel welcome and comfortable and to know that you are a professional concerned about doing what is best for the students, staff, and community. Making thoughtful design decisions can greatly increase the chances of that happening and assist you in becoming a savvy principal.

Chapter Thirteen

Playing the Visibility Game

One of the biggest challenges facing new principals, and an ongoing one for veterans, is feeling the need to meet the expectations of being everywhere, for everyone, all the time. There are days when being cloned wouldn't allow you (both of you) to be in all the places you need to be. You may have gone from a position of relative obscurity, although critical, to that of a power broker, whereby people now care about everything you say and do.

Teachers, parents, and students all want to see their principal in the corridors and cafeteria and at athletic events, plays, and concerts. They want to feel that their principal is accessible and supportive. You may even like the fact that everyone wants your attention, as it can be an ego boast. It is nice to feel wanted and valued.

I can remember sacrificing myself—and sometimes my family—in my determination to meet everyone's expectations. I needed to be the super principal that everyone expected me to be, or so I thought. I can also remember moments in my career when I wondered whether it made sense to keep trying to do what seemed impossible.

Did I have to be the first one at work and the last one to leave? Did I have to miss family events to watch other kids play games? Did I need to respond on weekends every time the building alarm went off? I remember a veteran high school principal telling me not to make the same mistake he did—raising everyone else's children but his own.

There just isn't enough time in the day to do all of the things that are expected of principals, let alone to attend a two-hour football game or theater production. You must file state and federal reports, conduct teacher evaluations, write recommendation letters, prepare budgets, assuage parents' feelings, and resolve staff conflicts. The items on the to-do list are never all crossed off. And, in addition to professional deadlines that have to be met, principals also have personal lives and obligations that cannot be ignored.

But most teachers still expect to see the principal in every corner of the building during the day; the director of the chorus still expects the principal to be at the evening concert; the girls on the basketball team still expect to see the principal at their game; and parents still expect to see the principal wherever their children are performing or competing.

So what do you do to balance the requirements of the job with personal and family responsibilities, because if you don't, one of these will suffer? And you don't want it to be your family.

First of all, before you accept the position, ask the superintendent what the expectations are of administrators, in particular you, for being at events that take place evenings and weekends. Don't be afraid to ask, thinking that if you ask you won't get the job. It does not indicate someone who doesn't want to work and be successful at the job but rather one who is mature and confident to ask key role expectations. If the expectations are more than you know you can meet, it is better to understand that up front.

Great superintendents to work with will respect your concern about meeting the needs of the position as well as your concern for your family. If they respond that you are expected to be at everything, find another position, as that one won't work. For the job to be rewarding for you, superintendents need to have values that are similar to yours. They will understand the job is demanding and at times requires long hours and sacrifices. They will also encourage you to put family first as many times as possible. If not, they know they will lose you.

I learned early in my career that I had to be at some events so teachers, parents, and students knew I cared about what they did. And I did very much enjoy watching them participate and perform. But what they didn't know is that, although I was there, I wasn't always there. I had learned to play the visibility game. So how did I play the visibility game?

I arrived at the school early each day, which was easy for me since I am a morning person. I would sit on a bench outside the main entrance, with a cup of coffee, and greet everyone. There were times when I may not have been at the school the rest of the day, but everyone saw me at least once.

During the school day, I made sure that I was in the corridors at times when I could see and be seen by as many teachers and students as possible. During passing time, I cruised the building, walking down corridors, poking my head into classrooms to greet teachers, stopping momentarily to chat with students, and trying to speak to students by name.

In the middle of the day, I stationed myself at major hallway junctions during passing time so teachers and students could see me and be reassured that I was "around." I would conduct business at the same time that I was "being seen." When passing time was over and the halls emptied, I went back to my office or to a specific classroom to observe what was happening. I would drop in to as many lunch periods as possible, chatting with teachers and students.

It is important for principals to be seen during the school day, but it is also important to support the artistic efforts of students and staff members at plays and concerts. I did not always have the time, professionally or personally, to sit through an entire two-hour concert or play, especially one I had already seen, so I would go to the production, hang around the entrance as parents arrived, and greet them as they entered.

Before the curtain went up, I would find some reason to walk down to the front of the auditorium to check a microphone wire or locate someone (whom I couldn't find), thereby ensuring that everyone in the audience knew I was there. But when the production started, if I simply did not have the time to stay, I either went to my office to do paperwork or I went home to my family.

Likewise, I often did not watch entire athletic competitions. In many instances, I would be there, more to be seen than to watch the event. I greeted parents and stayed until the game got under way and then did other things. But while I was at the game, I moved around as if campaigning for office. There were also times when I brought one of my children, and we would watch as much of the game as possible.

There are also instances when it is appropriate to let people know how many nights or weekends you have been out when asked if you can attend another event. For example, you could say "I would very much like to go, but I have been out three nights already and my children are wondering who their dad/mom is" or "If I go to this game tonight, who is going to watch my kids play?"

Done tactfully, it can serve multiple purposes. It will let people know how much you work and that you like to watch your students perform, but it also lets them know your kids matter too. Most parents, if you are sincere and honest, will not only respect you for saying it, they will admire you. Never apologize for putting your family first.

Over the years, I developed a reputation for being "everywhere" and attending "everything," and that public perception fed into a broader perception that I was accessible to and supportive of everyone in the school community. That perception, in turn, resulted in a "trust bank" among staff members, students, and parents from which I could draw when I inevitably made a bad decision or had to make a hard decision.

I learned to play the visibility game. And lest some new administrator reading this might think I was Machiavellian and insincere in my support of students and staff members, I really did care what my students were doing, and I enjoyed chatting with parents and being seen. But at the same time, I had a life of my own—including a family who also needed my time and support.

By playing the visibility game, I could meet the demands of my job and the needs of my family at the same time. If you fail to play this game well, you will eventually lose one or the other. And that is not a choice any savvy principal should have to make.

Chapter Fourteen

The Kiss of Death

The Kiss of Death has never been thought of as a good thing. Whatever its frame of reference, from Judas's kiss on Jesus's cheek to identify him to the guard to the fabled Mafia practice that a kiss from the don meant curtains for the receiver, the outcome is not optimistic. It's equally as horrific for principals when they do something that makes them lose their credibility with the staff and, ultimately, respect from the community.

Most times the dilemmas principals face are not the direct result of something they did or did not do. It is estimated by some that, at least 95 percent of the time, those dilemmas are the result of staff whose actions were not well thought out or were just plain stupid. But there are times when the only person responsible for doing something incredibly brainless is the principal. Here is a scenario that exemplifies what may end up being for the leader "the kiss of death."

Mike had recently accepted a position as high school principal in an area of the state where he grew up. His last position was as an assistant principal at a high school fifty miles away. As he already owned a home in a community only ten miles from his new job, he saw this as a way to cut down on his commute and not have to relocate his family. He was also happy that his children would not be attending schools in the same district that he would be working in.

He viewed this position as a positive move, both professionally and personally. He was getting the opportunity to be a high school principal, and he would not have to relocate his family to do so. The extra time he would gain by not commuting he could spend with his family or at his new job. All the important pieces seemed to be in place for him to be successful at work and home.

The school had endured three principals over the past five years. Each one had separate and legitimate reasons for not succeeding. One principal had gotten her degree from an online program and had difficulty relating to staff. She lacked the ability to develop strong relationships with anyone in the school or community.

The next principal dodged every decision that came his way and didn't seem to have a handle on what direction the school was headed. His most common response was "I'll get back to you," but he never did.

The third individual had been coaxed out of retirement to serve as an interim principal, and like most interims, nothing much happened except that purchase orders got approved. He was a well-liked person, but no forward progress was made.

When Mike applied for the position (he was actually asked to apply), it was hailed by teachers and parents as a good thing. After a couple of months on the job, the superintendent asked me to work with Mike as his mentor. He sensed that things were not going as well as planned at the high school.

Although parents seemed to be very pleased with the new leader, there were rumblings from staff that he had some teachers that were considered part of the "in group." More specifically, there were two male teachers, similar in age to Mike, that he seemed to spend more time talking with during the day than with any other staff members. It was also rumored that the three of them were also seen spending time outside school socializing.

The superintendent knew that if this was true it would compromise Mike's ability to lead. The superintendent had met with Mike on several occasions to discuss how things were going but never was able to sort this one out. The superintendent knew the best hope for the new principal was a mentor.

At the first meeting with me, Mike seemed very comfortable and welcoming. He appreciated the opportunity to have someone available to discuss difficult issues in a confidential manner. He realized the tremendous opportunity he had in this role and wanted to be successful. He also knew the superintendent proved that he wanted him to succeed by providing him with a mentor. Principal Mike also knew that none of his colleagues at other high schools had that support.

When we discussed the possible concern about "in groups," he was sincere and adamant that he was not deliberately or in any manner showing any teachers preferential treatment. He acknowledged that he had known a couple of staff for a long time but that in no way would hinder his ability to do the job. These teachers received no special teaching assignments or preferential duty schedules. He did not think he spent more time talking to them in the school than he did anyone else. He was perplexed and somewhat hurt by these innuendos.

Mike admitted that he had been hired to turn things around at the school, and because of this he had probably upset or angered a few staff members. He wondered whether it was just a couple of disgruntled staff trying to cause problems and undermine his authority. He knew that being in his role he would probably ruffle a few feathers, but he did not want to be perceived as a leader that played favorites. He was perplexed and concerned. Mike felt his integrity was being questioned unfairly. He truly believed he was trying to do his best in this new job and that he was being careful not to play favorites.

One way to get some insight into what a principal values is to observe what is in her or his office or on the walls. As he had been in the position for only a few months, his office was still a work in progress. He had only three hangings on his wall. There was a picture of his family, his framed master's degree from a local university, and a plaque with a picture of himself and two others. On this plaque were three men holding golf clubs (drivers to be precise) and engraved underneath were words related to winning some golf tournament at a club in the area. He must have been extremely proud of this accomplishment.

When I asked him to talk about what was on the wall, he talked enthusiastically about his family. He had a wife and two children and explained how important family was to him. He went on to say he worried about working too many hours and wondered aloud about the struggle to find the right balance between work and home. He talked about the fun things they did as a family and how he cherished that time.

He spoke about how the shorter commute to work had allowed him to have breakfast in the morning, something he previously was unable to do. There also had been evenings during the week when he could get home before his children went to bed and that still left time for him and his wife to catch up on their daily activities.

He was proud of the fact that he had completed his master's degree in less than three years working full-time. He knew it had been a strain on him and his family, but he needed to do it for certification purposes. The late nights working on assignments and having to attend weekday evening classes had cut into family time. He knew it had placed an added burden on his wife and children, but he knew things had been much better since he had earned his degree.

He also discussed how much he had learned in his program and how that knowledge had prepared him for this new role. Without that degree, he would not have the credentials or knowledge to assume the role as high school principal, a career move he had aspired to for a long time.

He then talked about the golf plaque that hung just to the right of his desk. His tone and mannerisms indicted he obviously liked playing golf and was proud of the trophy. He lamented the fact that there was a time when he was younger when he could play five times a week but was now restricted to a once-a-week golf league at an area club. He talked about how his game had deteriorated but that he still enjoyed getting out once a week. He also enjoyed the camaraderie that went with playing a round. He went on to talk about the other two individuals in the picture. Dave and Jamie: two friends from high school and current staff members in the building. Fore!

Let's see if we have this straight and understand the reasoning behind the selection of these photos. He has three things on his wall—a family picture, his framed master's degree, and a picture of himself and two staff members winning a golf tournament. Of all the things he could have chosen, he selected these three because they must be extremely important to him.

There are none of the standard hangings you find on the walls in principals' offices. For example, there are no pictures of students involved in a volunteer activity or winning a state championship, no school mission statement professionally printed, no inspirational saying from a deceased president such as "It is hard to fail, but it is worse never to have tried to succeed."—Theodore Roosevelt.

There are basic rules for office wall hangings. First a family picture or pictures is a standard requirement. It is an absolute essential. It does not matter whether it is your parents, spouse, significant other, or children. Any combination is acceptable. Something has to be there, period.

Diplomas are OK and can express credentials that are important to the students and community. Medical doctors hang them in their offices for a reason. What is not OK is to display endless plaques of recognition or honors that you have received. Some of those you get by just being in your role. What you don't want to make your office is a shrine to you. Being principal of a school is not about your accomplishments. It focuses the attention on how smart you may be, not how savvy you are. And there is a difference. Mike got only the family picture right.

I asked him to talk more about the golf plaque and what perception he thought staff members, parents, or students might have upon seeing that picture prominently displayed on his wall for all to see. Would it be reasonable for them to infer that playing golf was something he really liked to do in his leisure time? He said yes. Would it be reasonable for them to infer that he was good at golf? He said yes. Would it be reasonable for them to infer that the other two individuals in the picture were good friends because he was playing in a golf tournament with them?

He paused for a moment and said yes. Would it be reasonable for them to infer that if he were playing golf with them on his leisure time that they would get preferential treatment at work? After a much longer pause, he reluctantly agreed that it could be a reasonable conclusion but it wasn't fair. He emphatically stated that he did not give them preferential treatment; in fact he went out of his way not to treat them differently.

The subsequent discussion centered on the notion that people's perceptions of reality are often more powerful than reality. It did not matter what his intent was in placing the plaque on the wall. What mattered was others' interpretation of that plaque. If the other two individuals in the photo did not work at the school, it would not be an issue. Since he was already subject to some scrutiny for appearing to favor some staff, this was damaging evidence to support those claims. The picture had to come off the wall, and fast. Mike removed the plaque from the wall and placed it in his desk.

So what happened to Mike? I continued to work with this principal for a couple of years. He appreciated feedback on his performance, enjoyed reflecting on how he was doing, and welcomed ideas and strategies on how he could be more effective.

The two individuals in the photo served on the principal's advisory committee. They were positive teachers committed to making the school a better place for students. They were eager to do more than normally expected of staff to help students succeed. But there was still an uneasiness in meetings around their close relationship with Mike, which often interfered with the good ideas the teachers proposed.

Ultimately, Mike was never able to overcome the perception that he played favorites, that he had an in group. It was difficult to assess whether he actually did favor some staff over others. In the end, it did not really matter if he did. It only mattered that some staff thought he did and that perception got in the way of his ability to be seen as a leader who cared about what every teacher thought.

In reality, it is no different from what students might say about some teachers—that they play favorites. Real or imagined, this perception limits the teacher's ability to reach and impact all students. The same is true for school leaders. It limits their ability to reach and impact all staff in a positive manner

After two years at the school, Mike took a job at another high school, where by all accounts, he is very successful. At least that is the perception in the school and community. And in the life of the principal, that is what really counts.

Chapter Fifteen

If You Allow It, You Approve It

Principals are the gatekeepers of the values of the school and community. Everything that happens at school, every decision that is made, must have a reason that is supported educationally and is in the best interest of the students. Savvy leaders take this aspect of their positions very seriously.

When you become the leader, every decision you render is a powerful indicator of what you believe and value. Signing off on a budget item, for example, SMART Boards, means you believe they are useful to teaching effectively and you want to buy them, right? When you recommend that a new teacher receives a continuing contract or tenure, you have affirmed she or he is a good teacher and has the potential to be great and you want her or him to continue working in the school, correct?

When you suspend a student for using steroids, you are saying you strongly disapprove of students using performing-enhancing drugs to improve their competing, right? When you propose a new curriculum that intends to teach students ethics and responsible decision making, it is because you deem those as important skills students should possess, correct?

Every decision that you don't make is also a confirmation of your approval/disapproval of your actions or someone else's. If a decision was made prior to your taking the position and is currently in existence, that does not take you off the hook. Let's look at an simple example of this. The long tradition, although currently decreasing in popularity, is the practice of including class superlatives in yearbooks. Here are a few of the categories found recently in high school yearbooks:

- Most athletic
- Best personality
- Best smile

- Best dressed
- Born in the wrong decade
- Most likely to appear on the wall of the post office
- Best couple
- Most talkative
- Class flirt
- Easiest to take home to Mom
- Most changed since freshman year
- Teacher's pet
- Teacher's pest
- Most likely to succeed
- Most artistic
- Most argumentative
- Best eyes
- Most theatrical
- Class clown

My guess is that you would have a difficult time defending the inclusion of many of these categories. How do you think a child from a family that is struggling economically feels when you have categories such as "best smile" and "best dressed" when they know they cannot afford to win either? Is it your intention to recognize those students who have access to money and make those who may be living in poverty, either long term or situational because of recent family job losses, to feel less worthy in your eyes?

It would be reasonable to assume that most parents want their children to be free of dental disease and the only reason they don't go to the dentist is they don't have enough money or health insurance to do so. Most parents, if they had a choice, would want their children to have straight and white teeth.

Do you really believe your students need to dress expensively to be successful in school? As long as they meet the dress code standards in your school, does it matter to you what the label is on their clothes or the cost? Is it not more important to have clothes that are appropriate than clothes that are costly?

Do you really care about how perfect someone's teeth look? Should you not be more concerned with all students having access to dental care so they are free of the pain that comes with decaying teeth?

How would you respond if a parent asks you "What are the rubrics for class flirt and best couple?" or says "Frankly, I am surprised that you, as principal, would encourage my son to make romantic overtures toward other young adults." If an activity is included in the yearbook, you have approved it. Do you really want to encourage flirting and dating as a school activity?

You must be able to explain to students, staff members, and parents the reasons for existing practices, programs, and activities. "Tradition" is not a good answer if it is not in the best interest of the students and community.

Let me share with you another example to make that point.

When you first click on the high school's website, the first thing to catch your eye is a beautiful picture of the front of the school. The grounds are nicely manicured, projecting a lush green, weed-free lawn, with a blue sky framing the structure in the background. As other pictures cycle through, you see students dancing on the stage, a football player diving across the goal line, three students taking water samples from a pond, and two students framing a house. There is the usual brief welcome from the principal along with links to the school-year calendar and the daily announcements. Tucked between the pictures at the top and the principal's message is this: "34 percent of all XHS teens have . . ." It then asks you to click on it to find the answer. Upon clicking, you see "consumed alcohol in the past thirty days."

Under this startling revelation is a list of thirty-two resources categorized as general information: resources for teens, parents, and educators regarding prescription drug abuse and marijuana use to help concerned individuals address these issues. The message is strong and clear. At this school, we are very concerned about teen drug use and want to help all those in the community to help us deal with this issue. You have to admire a school that will not hide the data with fear that it may make the school look bad. Rather, they are up front and provide extensive information and resources. Bravo, you say. You have to be impressed.

School leaders need to be clear and consistent in articulating their beliefs and must always act in ways that support those values. Students, staff, and community should not have to guess how a leader feels about a significant core value or certain action, in this instance, teen drinking and drug abuse. To do otherwise leaves people wondering what the leader will not compromise on or, on the other hand, will yield to under the slightest form of pressure.

When visiting schools or looking at their websites, review printed and digital artifacts such as student and staff handbooks, parent information booklets, and yearbooks. Much can be gleaned about what a school values by what it chooses to publish for all to see. Important insights can be learned about administration and staff perspectives on responsible student behaviors if we examine written student codes of conduct or school discipline philosophies. In other words, what are the respectful behaviors students are expected to learn, and how will we encourage, support, and hold them accountable for those actions? The more congruent the parts are, the more likely the expectations will match the behaviors.

An interesting piece of unobtrusive data used to verify this belief is to look at what is allowed to be included as a senior superlative. Remember, no superlative with a student selected to match it would get in the yearbook without administrative approval. Need examples? Have you ever seen "best plagiarizer in the top 10 percent of the class" or "most likely to land in jail" as a superlative? You get the point. Whatever appears in the yearbook is there because it has been allowed, and if you allow it you approve it.

Imagine your surprise when you examine the yearbook of the school described above and find under the senior superlative section "Life of the Party" accompanied by a picture. In the picture are a boy and girl holding red plastic cups in each hand with large smiles on their faces. They appear to be in a casual, outdoor setting. What is in the picture that would give clues as to why they were voted "Life of the Party"?

Could it be what is in the plastic cups that would cause them to be happy and voted this sought-after recognition? If an adult poll were taken on what is in the cups, it could be safely assumed that most people, maybe close to 99 percent of the adult population, associate red plastic cups with drinking alcoholic beverages. Think how proud the school and the parents of these high school students must be. This honor bestowed on these two students is certainly something to proudly include on any college or work application.

Now here is the real confusion. The school places on the front page of its website the strong message about not drinking and the dangers associated with such behavior and then goes on to feature two kids who presumably drink. Not only do they drink, but they are also the best in the senior class at it. How seriously do you think the students would take the message on the website?

Being a streetwise and savvy principal means having the courage to examine traditions and practices to ensure that they are consistent with the beliefs of the school community and in the best interests of all the students. Sometimes these are in conflict with each other, and that is when the leader has to be courageous.

Students expect the principal to be the guardian of what is right and fair. Students believe that what happens at school—be it class superlatives or instructional practices—is done with the principal's full knowledge and approval. And why wouldn't they? You are the leader of the school.

Students expect you to be their advocate, especially those students who have no other advocate. So the bottom line is this—endorsing a new practice or allowing an existing one to continue means you approve of it. If you don't want that responsibility, then don't take the position. Too many students and adults are counting on you to do the right thing. Will they be able to count on you? If you are a savvy leader, they will.

Chapter Sixteen

Parents Are Your Best Friends

When it comes to how principals view the role they want parents/caregivers to have in schools, there appears to be no middle ground. Some principals enthusiastically welcome parents to be full partners in the process of educating their children and recognize how valuable the school/home connection is to the students' success. As such, they design opportunities, activities, and communication strategies for them to be purposefully involved in. Parents are referred to in a caring and respectful tone and are made to feel welcome in the life of the school. The principal believes parental involvement matters, and the parents know that.

Other principals treat parents as adversaries—at best avoided and at least marginalized. In these buildings, the primary function of parents is to raise money for the school and staff and the booster group concession stand but don't try to infiltrate the building/classroom during regular school hours. There is a condescending tone that implies the school knows best how to educate the student, and well-behaved parents know that. The parents' job is defined as being needed to support the school with money, serve as a source of cheap labor, and assist in a crisis. You may drop your children off in the morning and pick them up at the door later in the day, but don't come inside unless you are requested and allowed to do so. The principal believes parent involvement doesn't matter, and the parents know that.

Savvy principals realize that the behavior of parents, and their attitude toward the school, plays a significant role in influencing the success their children will have in school. They believe strongly that when parents are positively involved their children are academically successful, well behaved, and goal oriented and have positive attitudes toward themselves and the school. Parent involvement can run the spectrum from checking on homework to being involved in the classroom or serving on a school policy committee.

If we know that parent involvement is highly beneficial, why then do some principals not take full advantage of this great resource? What would cause them to act in a manner that is not productive for anyone? Why do they leave parents on the outside looking in? I think there are three reasons for this:

1. *The principals lack confidence in their own capacity as leaders.* They are not sure of their competence/ability to lead and view anyone from the outside as a potential threat to uncovering this. They are deeply concerned that if staff and students do not respect them, it will be observed and made known to the community. They worry that if parents are able to observe them directly interacting with students, they will see how comfortable or uncomfortable they are as leaders. They fear that if parents overhear an unflattering comment made by a staff member directed toward them that it may undermine their authority in the community. In short, they are afraid of being exposed for what they may be—insecure or incompetent. They feel that to protect themselves from being exposed there is no other choice but to restrict access.
2. *The principals are intimidated by a few teachers who warn of a repeat of horror stories (parents) of the past.* These teachers caution principals about the terrible and meddling parents whose only role has been to make teachers look bad by finding blunders and failures that they could report to their friends. They see parents as wanting to be in schools only to cause chaos and harm. The only way to prevent those parents from behaving badly is to banish all parents from the premises, even the good ones. This also serves to protect the principals from having to deal with those teachers who behave badly. There is no other choice but to restrict access.
3. *The school has no sense of direction or purpose.* There is no game plan for becoming a great school. In these buildings, no one seems to be on the same page; rather, what exists is a disparate collection of unconnected people and programs. There is no relationship between what happens in one room with what happens in another. Anyone who is in the building for even a short period of time can pick up on that. Not knowing where you are headed in a time of rapid change in education is not a good thing for principal leaders to be recognized for. There is no other choice but to restrict access.

The end result of all these actions are principals who have created a dysfunctional wall with a surrounding moat between the school and community. This body of water around the school has a false bridge that lets only those perceived as "friends of the school" across it. There is no other choice but to restrict access.

Savvy principals do not have walls and moats around their schools to keep parents out nor do they selectively determine who can enter and under what conditions. Whatever the level of active involvement, there are some things savvy leaders rely on and openly support and encourage parents/caregivers to do. What are those parental behaviors these principals expect? Savvy principals strongly support and provide assistance to parents who:

- Model the importance of getting an education. They show constant support for learning, both verbally and through their actions. These parents realize that they are their children's most important teachers and, at the same time, realize they are valuable partners with the school. They constantly model learning. They might read when their children are doing homework or take everyday occurrences and make them teaching/learning experiences. In many instances, the school provides lists of activities parents and children can do together.
- Send their children to school rested, well nourished, and ready to learn. They give them the most nourishing, well-balanced diet they can afford. In cases where that is not always possible because of finances, the school/community provides for those needs, be it breakfasts in the morning or a place to take a shower. They closely monitor their children's out-of-school activities and behavior.
- Provide a place, time, and supervision for their children to do homework. When that is not possible, the school/community provides before- or after-school places where students are supervised and tutored by caring adults. Sometimes this occurs at school in before- or after-school programs, while at other times community organizations such as the Girls and Boys Clubs or churches offer space. They teach the children organizational strategies for fulfilling school responsibilities.
- Ask for, and use, the advice of the professionals at the school. In addition, they share information on the out-of-school experiences that would be relevant and helpful for the school to know. These parents truly believe that they and the school have the children's best interest at heart and by working together the children will come out ahead.
- Follow the request that, if parents/caregivers have a concern about something at school, they do not discuss it in front of the children. They understand the adult decision-making process in schools and how to follow those procedures. The knowledge of who has the authority to make which decisions is a crucial piece of information principals provide parents.

- Stay involved in their children's education through high school graduation. They encourage their children to do their best, not necessarily to be the best.

Savvy principals do all they can to support parents in acting responsibly on behalf of their children. This support may come in the form of informational programs, accessibility to themselves and the staff, or resources in the form of services or such things as breakfast programs or other community resources the school has knowledge of and access to.

It is everyone's responsibility to make parents and the community partners in students' learning. It is not just the job of the principal. It is everyone's job in the community to assist in helping children grow and learn in a safe and supportive environment. It is their job to champion that it be everyone's job to help students.

There are many successful ways, which have worked for years, to involve parents in the life of the school: open houses, parent organizations, homecomings, science or academic fairs, fun days, volunteering in the classroom or computer lab, being on committees, painting scenery for the school play, raising money to purchase needed items, mentoring, or coaching, to name a few. All of these can work with the right planning and attitude on the part of the school. They can all engage parents and help them feel more connected to the school and their children. But there is one activity that works best to engage parents in the school.

If there is one thing principals must absolutely do to foster great relations between parents and themselves, it is to form a principal advisory council. If they do nothing else, they will still realize a huge payoff.

The best activity ever developed to engage parents in the education of their children and to have a public relations winner is parent/student exchange day. Let me create a scenario to help you understand what this is all about.

Vanessa, a parent, walks proudly to receive her diploma as a member of the graduating class of October 31, 2013. She had successfully completed one day as a middle school student. She had done her homework in math, ridden the school bus, eaten from the salad bar in the school cafeteria, played soccer in physical education, discussed the upcoming presidential election in history class, and thrown on the potter's wheel. She had also forgotten the combination to her locker and sought assistance from a couple of fourteen-year-olds as she attempted to navigate her way to the music room.

When the day was over, she shared with other parents her new appreciation for the students, teachers, and rigors of the curriculum. She was exhausted from the pace of the day, amazed at the enthusiasm and kindness of the students, proud of being able to answer a question in English class, and looking forward to next year when she could again be a middle school student for a day.

Andrew, Vanessa's son, got up early to get breakfast for the family. He made sure Mom had her homework, laptop, and portfolio for art class. He prepared lunches for his two younger brothers and walked them to the bus stop. He hurried back home to clean the breakfast dishes and get ready for work. Today he was going to his mom's job as a real estate broker.

What is going on here? Mother and son are switching roles in the annual parent/student exchange day. Once a year parents and students may exchange places for the day. The program is based on the premise that since the school and parents share mutual concern for the education of students it is logical that they develop a collaborative partnership. This partnership should create a situation that encourages two-way involvement and communication between home and school. It offers the opportunity for parents and teachers to get to know one another in a way that is not possible through general meetings and conferences. It also provides students and parents with an appreciation and new respect for each other's responsibilities.

This continual public relations feeder system—from the school, through the parents, to the community—creates a greater understanding of educational needs and initiatives. Together, parents and teachers help each other to help students. It reinforces the belief that parents and teachers need to work together in the best interest of students. Parent/student exchange day epitomizes that partnership.

For students, understanding the world of work and being provided with opportunities to experience a variety of career options is an important component of increasing aspirations. Students need to explore the range of possibilities through research, discussions, projects, and participation at employment sites. Parent/student exchange day allows students to experience a vocation firsthand.

The key to a successful day is to do nothing out of the ordinary; classes should proceed as usual. If there is a quiz or exam scheduled, it is not rescheduled. If students are required to make a presentation in a group, parents participate. If an experiment is called for in science, parents make an attempt. If Zumba is the activity of the day in health, parents join in.

All that is really needed is willingness on the part of staff to cooperate. There is a natural anxiety on the part of some staff members that they are onstage and might mess up. The principal can hold the same fear. Those who work with students know that even the best plans don't always work and that anything is possible. Truth be told, most parents are far more nervous about making a mistake than are the staff members. A key is to let the parents be a part of that spontaneity. If there is genuine trust between the staff and administration, there is no way this is not a public relations winner for both.

To make the day work, teachers must assign homework the day before. This creates the necessity for cooperation and communication between parents and children. For some parents and children, discussing homework may not be commonplace. This one activity that can open the door to a more healthy relationship and more dialogue between parents and children. If this occurs, both benefit. Students need to provide their parents with the schedule they will follow and the materials they will need to make it through the day.

Students who exchange places with their parents must do just that. To experience the demands of a career or running a household, a job description form must be completed. In this document are the educational requirements, skills required, and typical work schedule. Students also keep journals on their activities to reflect on what they have learned and how the day may have helped with a career decision.

If students are working at home that day, they may initially see the day as an opportunity to sleep late and have fun. Instead, they will find themselves getting up earlier than everyone else to make breakfast and get the children off to school or safe. Students are usually surprised at what it means to stay inside and work all day. They gain a new appreciation for those who work at home.

The role of the school is critical in making the day a success. Well in advance of the first time this day is offered, the school needs to provide news releases and notices to businesses. The groundwork here is key to getting parents released from work without losing income. Making the community aware of the goal of the activity and acquiring their support is crucial to the day's success. All staff members should be well informed so they can respond to the interest and excitement this program will create. After the first year, the program publicizes itself through the enthusiasm of previous parent participants.

With thoughtful and diligent planning, support from staff, and cooperation from the community, this program is an absolute winner. Following are some of the tangible benefits this program offers:

1. *Increased student/parent understanding and communication.* One of the major benefits is the increase in dialogue between parents and children. This activity provides a structure for talking about school and home and opens doors for additional sharing on other issues. Parents have told me that this format has provided a wonderful opportunity for them to better know their children through an understanding of the world they are experiencing, especially their friends, schoolwork, and pressures. Students often comment that their parents better understand the pressures they face in school and how busy their schedules are in and out of school.

2. *Information about careers and future opportunities.* Students get to experience, firsthand, a career for a day. Through the research they do, they learn what it takes to get and keep a job. They gain not only a new level of awareness of a particular career but a deeper understanding of their parents' work world. The subsequent sharing in the classroom allows more students insight into a number of career areas and provides real-life application of book knowledge.
3. *Better understanding of what current schooling is all about.* Most parents attended schools that were drastically different from the ones today. Misperceptions are clarified, and parents learn the depth and scope of the curricula and the opportunities available to students. The best way to learn the mission of a school today is to experience it from the perspective of a student.
4. *Increased support for school and staff by parents and the community.* If you allow parents in to observe how the school works, it is perceived as being an open, honest place where they are welcome. Staff members are appreciated for their hard work, willingness to take risks, and the caring they demonstrate in the classrooms. The business community recognizes the school's efforts in preparing students for the future, which can also lead to more school/business partnerships.
5. *School and community morale booster.* This is a fun activity. Initial anxiety, on the part of parents and staff, diminishes soon after the school day begins. Everyone has a good time experiencing school in the twenty-first century. Positive comments flow in the school and community. Everybody talks about it. Everybody wins.

A fundamental need of today's society is cooperation within the broad community known as education. School systems that are strong will find administrators, teachers, parents, and students engaging in a mutual effort to make the process work. Parent/student exchange day is a viable activity that addresses this need for respectful cooperation. Positive feelings about education and educators are reinforced as a result. Savvy principals know that when that occurs everyone wins.

Chapter Seventeen

How to Become a Savvy Principal

Savvy principals do not work alone or in isolation from others. They do not make all or even most of the important decisions. In fact, the fewer decisions they make should be a reflection of others taking more ownership.

Building an organizational structure that changes the decision-making process is not as simple as adding a new program to the curriculum. It is about changing how people interact, how decisions are made and by whom, how people utilize their time, how differences get heard and addressed, and how the principal interacts with students, staff, parents, and community members.

For some teachers, being able to make significant decisions is a total departure from their experiences working in schools. With more and more mandates from the local, state, and federal level, it is becoming increasingly foreign to their experiences, even in schools that have attempted to be more collaborative.

Sadly, we have also done a good job of educating parents that most schools are not shared places of inquiry or decision making. For example, beginning in elementary schools, most parents become conditioned to call the principal if they have a question. As a result of this contact, they expect a decision to be made and made quickly and unilaterally.

When they are told that their question is best answered by someone else or by a team of teachers, parents often become frustrated, wonder who is in charge, and question the principal's ability to make decisions or be in control of the school. They may even wonder what the principal is doing and think that, if the teachers are making all the decisions, then a principal may not even be necessary.

Becoming a leader of a collaborative school is not a simple task. If that were the case, more would be doing it effectively. The process begins with a principal who actually believes in collaboration.

Take the quiz in table 17.1 to determine whether you are ready to step up and become the savvy leader of a collaborative school. Answer each question honestly. No one is watching nor will the results be publicized. Respond to each statement by circling either strongly agree (SA), agree (A), disagree (D), or strongly disagree (SD).

Let's examine what your responses mean.

Table 17.1.

1.	The principal is in the best position to make all the major educational decisions in the school.	SA	A	D	SD
2.	Teachers' time is better spent teaching rather than doing administrative tasks.	SA	A	D	SD
3.	Teachers should play a significant role in decision making.	SA	A	D	SD
4.	Regarding school policy, operations, and curriculum, teachers neither want nor need additional responsibilities.	SA	A	D	SD
5.	The time the principal spends developing a collaborative workplace is not worth the payoff.	SA	A	D	SD
6.	Teachers would rather be told what to do than participate in decisions impacting them.	SA	A	D	SD
7.	Teachers want to make decisions but don't want to accept the responsibility for the decisions.	SA	A	D	SD
8.	Most teachers prefer to work alone rather than with other professionals.	SA	A	D	SD
9.	The principal must be a collaborative leader to be streetwise and savvy.	SA	A	D	SD
10.	Collaborative teams in schools reduce the power of the principal.	SA	A	D	SD
11.	Developing high-performing team structures requires training and resources.	SA	A	D	SD
12.	Collaboration sounds good, but at my career stage it's just not worth the effort.	SA	A	D	SD

1. If you answered agree or strongly agree, you are out of touch with reality, and the only reason you are holding on to your job is because you work for a superintendent that believes as you do. When he or she leaves, your best career move would be to retire. Your era as a leader has ended, even if you do not know it.

2. Your answer depends on your definitions of teacher and principal. If you feel that teachers should have significant input into decisions that impact their work, then collaboration will work. If you believe that the only decisions teachers should make are those within their classrooms, then it won't work.
3. If you believe that principals should expand the number of people who make decisions that impact the entire school beyond one (yourself), then collaboration will work. If you disagree with the statement, then attempting teaming will only make matters worse. The school may not be working well now, but at least the roles of teacher and principal are understood. All people know their places, including students and parents. If you try to change this structure and only superficially or halfheartedly make an attempt at meaningfully involving others, teachers will know you have manipulated them. They may even become angry that you made this insincere attempt. Even worse is that you will ruin it for the next principal who desires to build a collaborative school, as teachers will be mistrustful of repeated attempts since their only experience was a bad one.
4. Great teachers want to have an influence on their work life. In fact, can you think of people in any profession in any field that do not want to have significant control over their work? It is wrong to assume that teachers will not take on additional responsibilities that will improve their performance and job satisfaction. What teachers don't desire is additional work that consumes time and results in nonproductive outcomes.
5. It takes significant time, energy, and resources on the part of the principal to develop high-performing teams. It is much easier and takes less time to have the principal make all the decisions. But it is not better. It is also a huge mistake to construct and announce some sort of team structure and declare victory. Since working together is a foreign concept to most staff, there must be a heavy investment of time and money in training. Until recently, there were very few teachers who had experienced a group paper or project in undergraduate or graduate school. Therefore, to assume they know how to work together productively on significant high-stakes work is a mistake. Can you imagine having an athletic team at your school that did not practice between games? No coach would last long if he or she just told the students to show up for the games. Unfortunately, too many principals have made that mistake with staff. A streetwise and savvy principal knows the investment that is required to take full advantage of the skills teachers bring to the school each day. Investing in teachers' skills will contribute significantly to building a culture in the building receptive to change and innovation.

6. If you marked agree or strongly agree, you are either totally consumed by your own perceived greatness or out of touch with the professionalism of today's teacher. Or maybe both. In any case, if this statement accurately reflects your thinking at this point in your career, little will change your mind.
7. The answer to this question is yes and no. It really depends on whether teachers trust the principal. Trust in this situation means that the teachers sincerely believe that the principal is being honest regarding collaboration. If there is a genuine sense of we (rather than teachers versus principal), teachers will accept responsibility for their decisions. It is also important that the work they are being asked to do be seen as important work. Having the opportunity to influence curriculum decisions and instructional strategies is more apt to gain buy-in than being asked to select the menu at staff development days. Unless teachers feel they have a meaningful stake in determining and carrying out the game plan, they will not assume any responsibility for the outcome of the game.
8. If you believe that becoming educated is to a large degree based on learning how to develop relationships, then there is no way that you could think that teachers want to work alone. Maybe you like working alone and assume because of that everyone wants to work alone. I will grant you that there are some teachers who do prefer to work alone. There are also professions where working independently most of the time is the mode of operation. Education is not one of those professions. The challenges facing schools today are too complex and demanding to be solved by having teachers and principals working in isolation from each other.
9. This is not a trick question. Again, if you don't strongly agree with the statement, consider once again putting down this book. The fact that you have not quit at this point means you are at least considering the idea. I encourage you to keep reading. What do you have to lose?
10. Power is not finite. It does not add up to 100 percent. In actuality, the less you have to use your influence to make decisions, the more power you actually gain. If you ever worry about losing power as a principal, in reality you probably have already lost what little authority you had. If you believe there is only so much power to go around and that if you give some away (share) that your role is somehow diminished, then forget teaming. Streetwise and savvy principals realize that the job of principal as currently defined is too large for one person to accomplish. They understand that meaningfully involving others in the decision-making process greatly enhances their actual role power. If staff members have the authority to make legitimate and important deci-

11. You must invest in your staff. Training must be ongoing, comprehensive, and responsive to the needs and questions of teachers. Anything less than full commitment to doing this guarantees failure or, at the very least, increased frustration and disappointment on the part of staff. Without the commitment to training, resources, and risk taking, nothing will change. Don't ask people to change without providing them with opportunities to learn the new skills/behaviors required of them in their new roles.
12. The answer to this is self-evident. You are both streetwise and savvy, or you're not.

So if there is agreement that savvy principals lead collaborative schools, then how do principals go about making that happen? There is no one blueprint for these structures or one-size-fits-all model. There are, however, some clear aspects that must be present. To begin, a clear sense of mission, closely aligned with an articulate plan of direction, is the key to a successful collaborative school organization. If staff members do not know the focus and direction of the school, then there will always be arguing over what that should be. Without that common understanding, individual time and talents are wasted, and no real work gets completed. In addition, it is essential that high and realistic expectations for students and staff be established and monitored. There are some key elements of a productive organization.

First and foremost, each person should be viewed as a professional individual and an individual professional. The leader must sincerely value and respect the knowledge and talents that each person brings to the school, realizing that it is the effective utilization of those skills and talents that makes the school high performing. Staff brains should not be left in the parking lot.

The principal does not have all the answers to the challenges presented, but the collective wisdom of the staff may, if structured properly. It is the primary role of the principal to find the uniqueness in all staff members and to encourage them to share it for the good of the system and themselves.

Second, those who work in the building need an organizational structure that allows for flexibility, creativity, and accountability. The school must be organized in a way that requires collaboration, while at the same time does not remove the opportunities for individuals to shine. The group cannot be more powerful than the individual. If teachers feel that there is no opportunity for them to be themselves, they will soon lose their sense of identity. There needs to be balance.

Professionals need control over their work environment. For example, it would be unwise to have a curriculum that mandated specific teaching strategies that needed to be followed every period, every day. I am familiar with a school that does just that, and the turnover rate for faculty is very high. Teaching is not just a science but an art. For students to grow and prosper, it is important that they encounter a variety of teaching styles and methods.

It is common in middle school or on freshman teams to assign a team of teachers the task of designing how they would schedule the instruction for their students. Could they have longer blocks of time on specific days to do integrated curriculum work?

Is it necessary to schedule math five days a week, or could students have it three days a week for longer periods of time? Could teachers be trusted to make those decisions while still adhering to local and state mandates?

The recognition and full appreciation by the principal for work done by others in the building is essential. The recognition must be specific, genuine, and timely. In all my years as an administrator, I never had one staff member ask me to stop telling him good things about his performance. Likewise, I never had a student tell me to talk to her teacher and ask the teacher to stop giving her praise.

What I did learn was that my best staff members wanted frequent interactions with me, actively seeking my perspective on what they were doing and how they could do better. It is human nature to want to do a good job and to be appreciated for it. For some unexplained reason, too many leaders do not understand that.

Professional development must meet the needs of every person in the building as well as support the direction the organization is headed. There must be congruency in a well-planned and well-thought-out program. With time and resources in short supply in schools, neither can be wasted on ill-conceived professional development. There should be a plan developed that is updated each year and approved by the central office and/or school board. The focus should always be on what new learning the organization can provide its members to further the development of the organization as well as its members. They must be parallel.

And, finally, any organizational structure must be based on the assumption that working together, rather than in isolation, leads to greater job satisfaction and productivity. It has been my experience that the least stressful times of day for teachers and administrators are when they are working together finding solutions to common teaching and learning problems or when they are working together to solve schoolwide issues.

The problems that schools have to address each day are too difficult for any individual working alone to solve. It is also more fun to work with a group of people who value and recognize the talents each member brings to the school setting. The leader must recognize and validate the belief that for each staff member to be successful, everyone must work together.

Savvy principals recognize that although everyone may have different positions in the building, everyone is equally responsible for ensuring that the students get the best possible education. In a highly functioning organization, everyone is as important as everyone else. There are just different job titles.

With that framework in place, develop a clear definition and understanding of what it means to be a collaborative school and who makes what decisions in that structure. Too many schools form teams and don't know why they did. Don't think that is true? Next time you are at a conference, ask these questions of people who say they work in teams in their school:

1. Why do you have teams in your school?
2. What were the reasons you went to teaming?
3. What will be better for students, staff, and parents as a result of your teaming efforts?
4. What important decisions do you now make that you did not make before teaming was implemented?
5. How will you know whether teaming is working?
6. How is your work life different?
7. What professional development/training did you receive to become a team player?

Chances are that you won't need to go beyond question #1 before you realize that there are problems. If people can't give you specific reasons for teaming, then there is little hope that the efforts will work. Answering why is the critical question. Similar to the student asking why he or she needs to learn this information, teachers need to know why they are being asked to alter the working structure in the school.

Schools are complex organizations that have to work to fulfill their mission. In the past, the tasks to complete the work requirements of the system were hierarchically delineated, with groups and individuals doing specific functions. Management (central office mostly, principals occasionally, and school boards too frequently) made the most important decisions regarding budgeting, staffing, curriculum, and, in some instances, instructional strategies. The workers (teachers always and principals sometimes) were required to carry out those mandates.

Although some would argue that work relationships are clearer and less complicated in that structure, dissatisfaction with that model has led to more widespread attempts at more collaborative schools. Although schools began attempts at teaming in the 1960s with Lloyd Trump's model schools project, it has been only in the past thirty years that we have seen sustained growth in this effort.

Most successful businesses realize that to economically compete, they need to more effectively and efficiently involve the workers in the decision-making process. So too have progressive schools. No longer can they afford to have their employees not be fully contributing members.

Savvy companies realize that unless the workers have some stake in the outcome, the product will be continually inferior and expensive to produce. In addition, the loyalty factor is missing. By and large, those companies that have been willing to involve the employees in decisions that were previously made by management and have invested the necessary resources to train them have prospered.

Schools have also begun to more aggressively pursue collaboration as a form of decision making but not to the same degree as businesses. The commitment has not been as well thought out or financially supported. It has been more rhetoric than reality. The good news is that we have some schools that have been very successful at teaming and we can learn from what they did.

The collaborative model you develop to do the work of the school is secondary to believing as the leader in the importance of adults working together. There are many successful models that streetwise and savvy principals utilize.

Although a school may be collaborative in structure, that does not imply that all decisions are made jointly. What decisions administrators will decide unilaterally, what items will be decided in consultation with teachers, and what issues will be decided by teachers without consultation with administrators are important items to determine. Also, look at what role students and parents will play in the process. Collaboration does not always mean democratic decision making.

Savvy principals realize that leading successful schools is a complex undertaking that requires all the players—students, teachers, parents, administrators, and community members alike—to have a real investment in the outcomes. They understand that for people to have a meaningful stake in the outcomes requires that they must have significant roles in making decisions impacting those outcomes. Setting up structures whereby all those constituents feel ownership in the process and a responsibility for those outcomes is the job of the principal.

If you play in the game, you are likely to want to win the game more than someone who sits on the bench and watches. The obvious reason for that is that you have a real stake in the outcome. Others are depending upon you to contribute. You are not a spectator.

In our schools today, there are unfortunately too many spectators and not enough players. Too many people who can help students be successful are on the sidelines. Principals who make a difference expand the human resource base. They know how to get people to commit to and identify with the school and its success.

Savvy principals understand that the challenges schools face are too comprehensive and difficult to be the sole responsibility of the principal working alone. They also understand there are times they need to act in ways that are nonconventional, taking risks that are sometimes questioned, yet always acting in a thoughtful and strategic manner.

More important, these principals are not looking to receive accolades for their work or put plaques on their office walls. Their satisfaction comes from watching others succeed and get recognized. At the end of the day, that is what actually makes them savvy principals.

About the Author

Jody Capelluti is a professor of educational leadership at the University of Southern Maine. Prior to teaching at USM, he held a number of positions including teacher, principal of a National School of Excellence, director of special services, director of elementary education, director of curriculum, director of alternative programs, and planning associate at the Maine Department of Education.

As a scholar, he has coauthored four books and written approximately fifty articles and chapters in the areas of principal leadership, middle-level education, and school change. He is a consultant to schools in the areas of principal mentoring, school change initiatives, staff assessment and evaluation, and organizational development. He currently works as a coach to administrators in schools that are attempting significant changes in how they are organized and deliver instruction.

www.ingramcontent.com/pod-product-compliance
Lightning Source LLC
Chambersburg PA
CBHW031713230426
43668CB00006B/198